THE GOLD SOVEREIGN

MICHAEL A. MARSH

MICHAEL A. MARSH (PUBLICATIONS)
25A ST NEOTS RD
HARDWICK
CAMBRIDGESHIRE
CB3 7QH

FIRST EDITION (The Gold Sovereign 1760-1980) 1980.
SECOND EDITION (The Gold Sovereign 1489-1999) 1999.

Printed and bound in the United Kingdom
at the University Press, Cambridge

ISBN: 0 9506929 3 X

CONTENTS

PREFACE

Since I wrote and published *The Gold Sovereign* in 1980 a period of close on twenty years has passed by, and during this time new types and varieties have appeared within the currency series of the sovereign. Some of these were drawn to my attention by correspondents, and also by some who deal in coins; to both I am most grateful. With this help and also the examination of many more sovereigns it has become obvious to me that I must write a new and updated edition of *The Gold Sovereign*.

Apart from the new types and varieties I have just mentioned, and they are from years gone by, the reign of our present Queen Elizabeth II has moved on over the same period of time, consequently in this area also new gold coins have been struck, probably most important of these being the gold Proof Sovereign to mark the 500th Anniversary in 1989.

The format of the second edition will be the same as the first book of 1980, and also the same rarity ratings. However, in this edition I have decided to include the 'Australian' Sydney Mint sovereigns of 1855-1870, both types, and because I do not wish to disrupt the numbering system of the first book this new entry will be numbered to follow on after the Elizabeth II coins. One has to remember that some 6000 copies of the first edition exist and I felt that their existing numbering system should be protected. The new types and variations earlier mentioned will be added to the existing numbers simply by the use of A, B, or C etc. Another point I would ask you to note is that of the rarity ratings, and scrutiny of these will reveal that some changes have been made. I will simply say 'Father Time' was again responsible for these alterations.

Another important change I have felt necessary is in the Preface you will see I begin with the Reign of Henry VII; this I realized was necessary quite simply because since my first publication in 1980 many people have asked how and when the coin got its name. Of course these questions were only answerable by going back in time, and the answers are to be found in the reign of Henry VII. There had always been some divergence of opinion as to which of the coins from the reign of Henry VII was the first to bear the name of the sovereign. It gives me great pleasure to tell you that these questions were answered very well by our own Professor of Numismatics here in Cambridge, Professor Philip Grierson.

In this new edition, the text I have increased to around 30,000 words; it contains an enlarged historical content, and also much more about the important part played by the Royal Mint throughout this particular period of time.

A number of new plates are included, several of which are in colour, and I am sure you will enjoy the Electron Scanning Microscope pictures that produce such fantastic detail.

As far as rarity and availability are concerned I have given a rating for every sovereign listed; this rating is based on sovereigns found in very fine condition but it must be remembered that many of the common sovereigns become much rarer if found in uncirculated grade.

C	Common
N	Normal
S	Scarce
R	Rare
R2	Very Rare
R3	Extremely Rare
R4	15 to 25 examples known
R5	9 to 14 examples known
R6	4 to 8 examples known
R7	Highest rarity possible

ACKNOWLEDGEMENTS

My interest in the wonderful hobby of coins now goes back to almost forty years and during this time I have written many papers and have just finished this my fifth book. Throughout this period I have been fortunate to make many friends and acquaintances in the coin world, and often more than one has been willing to assist for which I am most grateful. But in this short list of acknowledgements I want to make a special mention of two people, and they are Graham Dyer of the Royal Mint and Maurice Howard a member for many years of the Cambridgeshire Numismatic Society. I have known both for a great number of years during which time they have contributed greatly to my interest in coins and in writing. Their assistance and advice always readily, no matter when. To Graham and Maurice I say thank you so very much.

The Royal Mint

The British Museum, London

The Fitzwilliam Museum, Cambridge

Mr F. Bird (Photographer)

Mr G. P. Dyer, Librarian and Curator, Royal Mint

Mr M. F. Howard

Mrs M. Story

Mr S. Warren

Dr R. S. Paden (Electron Optics Ltd)

MICHAEL A. MARSH

LIST OF ILLUSTRATIONS

THE ORIGINAL SOVEREIGN

Many students of modern British gold are aware of when the first ever sovereign was introduced to our coinage, but as I mentioned in my Preface I have had many inquiries from others who quite obviously wanted to know the answer, and this prompted me to begin this second edition with the reign of Henry VII where the question is answered.

We know that during the reign of Henry VII there were in fact five different gold coins struck during this reign called sovereigns, and we are indebted to a fine paper by Professor Philip Grierson that was published in the *British Numismatic Journal* of 1964 and reveals much about these coins.[1] It also tells us which was the earliest, and so in fact the first of our gold coins to bear the name of sovereign. This query had of course arisen because none of the five types struck bore a date, as was usual in the fifteenth century.

The period of some 500 years before Henry VII had a coinage that consisted almost entirely of silver pennies, and their weight was such that 240 of them equalled one pound and became known as the pound sterling. During this period other attempts were made to establish a gold coinage and in 1344 Edward III issued the gold florin with a value of 6s. but this was soon superseded by the noble valued at 6s. 8d., and this was accompanied with halves and quarters. In 1465 the noble was replaced by the angel also valued at 6s. 8d., and the ryal of 10s. with halves and quarters also issued. It was time the public were given the choice of a much higher value gold coin than they had ever before had available to them, and the new English sovereign came into existence by a commission dated 28 October 1489. This instructed the Mint to strike a gold double ryal worth 20s. to be called the sovereign, and two sovereigns were to be struck from every pound of Tower metal (proportion of 1 in 11 ¼) and the design was to be according to a print of lead attached to the Letters Patent. The sovereign (Plate No 1) marked a new era in the English coinage both in its size and because for the first time the pound sterling was presented as a single coin. [2]The obverse of the sovereign features the King seated facing on a Gothic throne and holding in his hands an orb and sceptre. The legend is HENRICUS DI GRACIA REX ANGLIE ET FRANC DNS IBAR. The reverse was a large double rose having on it the royal escutcheon bearing the arms of France and England quarterly, and surrounded by the legend IHS AUTEM TRANSIENS PER MEDIUM ILLORUM IBAT.

The Mint engraver at this time was Michael Flynt and so it is likely that the new sovereign was his design and work. However it must be noted that the

---

1. Professor Philip Grierson, 'The Origin of the English Sovereign and the Symbolism of the Closed Crown', *British Numismatic Journal.* London 1964, pp 118-134.
2. Courtesy of Trustees of The British Museum.

new coin appears to have been at least partly copied from an earlier gold coin of the Netherlands, the real d'or of Maximillian King of the Romans, as regent for his son Philip the Handsome in 1487. When one looks at the plates shown in Professor Grierson's paper on the two coins then it is not difficult to recognize a number of similarities between them. But without doubt it must be said the sovereign described is rich in beauty and is a magnificent example of the Tudor period, and it is also of the highest rarity because it is the only known example of its kind. Since 1915 the coin has been in the British Museum collection.

Sovereigns were struck by each successive monarch until after the accession of James I when their production ceased until 1817.

HENRY VII

Plate 1.

Obverse and Reverse of the Henry VII Sovereign 1489

GEORGE III 1760-1820

The death of George II on 25 October 1760 saw his grandson succeed to the throne as George III, and the gold coins in use were the guineas, half guineas, third guineas, and quarter guineas.

The guinea was undoubtedly the major coin of the eighteenth century but far more often than not it encountered long periods of troubled times;[1] these included the withdrawal of huge quantities of guineas that had been in circulation far too long and so were very light in weight. In 1793 war broke out with revolutionary France resulting in large quantities of gold leaving our resources during this long war, and also during this time a similar situation arose with Spain that yet again caused revenue problems. Inevitably, gold was hoarded and its place was taken by banknotes of one pound and two pounds.

However, the guinea was to soldier on and so we move to probably one of the most important dates of Royal Mint history,[2] and this was 6 July 1812. On this day William Wellesley Pole was appointed Master of the Mint, and he came from a remarkable Irish family of which the great Duke of Wellington was the third of four brothers. The eldest of these being the Marquis of Wellesley, and the second was William Wellesley who later became Wellesley Pole in acknowledgement of a legacy. Pole had previously held the position of Clerk to the Ordnance, Secretary to the Admiralty, and Secretary for Ireland. He was given the appointment with specific orders to completely re-organise the Mint, and later he was to be responsible for the introduction of the new coinage.

Pole very soon discovered just how bad the present situation was, and in fact it had become almost impossible to maintain the existing currency system. It was quite obvious that something must be done, and a Privy Council Committee on Coin recommended a new gold coinage of ten-shilling, twenty shilling, forty-shilling and five-pound pieces, and this was approved by the Prince Regent on 3 August 1816.

The new sovereigns, given currency by a Royal Proclamation of 1 July 1817, were struck for the first time later that year, so the modern sovereign as we know it today was born. The new sovereign and half-sovereign replaced the guinea and third guinea.

In the meantime important changes were happening at the Mint in respect of the engraving staff. Lewis Pingo,[3] the English Chief Engraver was retired, and he had been Chief Engraver since 1779. Nathaniel Marchant the Frenchman who was Second Engraver had reached the age of 76, and because of failing health he too was retired. Thomas Wyon was given the post of Chief Engraver

---

1. G. P. Dyer, 'The Modern Sovereign' (3) *Royal Sovereign* 1489-1989, Royal Mint 1989, pp 41-43.
2. Sir John Craig K.C.V.O., LLD. 'William Wellesley Pole', *The Mint* Cambridge 1953, pp 278-289.
3. C. Eimer, *The Pingo Family & Medal Making in 18th Century Britain*. London 1998.

and William Wyon became Second Engraver. At this point I must mention another person who was to be appointed to the engraving staff, and his name was Benedetto Pistrucci, a fiery little Italian, but without doubt a unique engraver.

I quote a letter written to the Treasury on 19 June 1816 by William Wellesley Pole,[1] Master of the Mint, "I have thought it desirable to employ Mr. Pistrucci, an artist of the greatest celebrity and whose work places him above all competition as a gem engraver, to make models for the dies of the new coinage and I request your lordships authority to pay Mr. Pistrucci such remuneration as may be necessary for his works. It is my intention that the models of Mr. Pistrucci should be engraved in Jasper from which our engravers will work in Steel and the models will be deposited in the Royal Mint and remain with the Dies and Proof Impressions of the several coins." Pistrucci had been introduced to Pole by Sir Joseph Banks, President of the Royal Society and a most influential person in very high places. The appointment of Pistrucci was confirmed on 26 June 1816, and although Pole had wanted to employ him as the Chief Engraver he could not do so because Pistrucci was in fact an alien, therefore he could not officially be given the top position. To overcome this he was in fact employed as an outside assistant and Thomas Wyon continued as Chief Engraver.

Wyon in fact died on 22 September 1817 and Pole wanted Pistrucci to occupy Wyon's position. However, due to circumstances I have already described this was not possible, but a loophole was found that allowed Pistrucci to take over all of Wyon's duties, but not that of his official position. In this area the Mint official records were in fact left blank, and remained so until 1828 when William Wyon became Chief Engraver. So Pistrucci was to carry out all the duties of Chief Engraver, provide all models and engrave all dies, and his salary was £500 a year. William Wyon remained Assistant Engraver to Pistrucci.

Before the death of Thomas Wyon Pistrucci had already been involved in the preparation of the new coinage, and he had engraved a cameo of the King's head in Jasper, to serve as a model for the sovereign, shilling and sixpence. The second Jasper cameo was a similar piece, and he then cut a third Jasper cameo of the King's head to serve as a model for the half-crown. Finally he produced a model in wax of St.George slaying the Dragon to serve as a model for the reverse of the crown. For these four works Pistrucci was paid £312.8s. Pistrucci himself suggested that his wax model of St.George should be used for the new gold coinage, and as a result of this he was asked to produce a model; for this work he was paid the sum of one hundred guineas. He was

---

1. M.A. Marsh, *Benedetto Pistrucci Principal Engraver & Chief Medallist of The Royal Mint* 1783-1855. Cambridge 1996 pp 16-17.

eventually asked to engrave both obverse and reverse dies of the new coinage, this being because the Mint engravers had failed to copy Pistrucci's models with much success. So the first of our modern sovereigns bearing the date of 1817 must be fully credited to the work and ingenuity of Benedetto Pistrucci. (Plate No. 2).

From the numismatist's point of view sovereigns of George III are becoming more difficult to find in really nice condition, and of the common dates any above the grade of E.F. will probably cost the collector from £500 upwards.

Without doubt the rarest coin in this series is that of 1819, and as I mentioned in 1980 I could only recall one sovereign of this date after many years searching. This piece had been holed and was generally in poor condition, so nearly 20 years have passed and it seems that only two more examples of this sovereign have appeared. The best of these was in fact last year on 15 and 16 October when Sotheby's of London held a fine Coins,[2] Medals and Banknotes Auction in London. Lot No.286 featured the 1819 Sovereign and in G.V.F. condition, it was indeed a fine specimen and probably the best of the six coins that are known to exist. The hammer price was an incredible £50,000 (Plate No. 3). This coin deserves a higher rarity rating in view of what we now know, and so I would ask you to note that it is now shown with a rating of R.6. This coin must be regarded as one of the rarest within the whole sovereign series.

You will see that for the year 1818 I now list three new varieties as Nos. 2A, B and C and these have obviously resulted from die changes, but they have appeared and so are included. I also include another interesting variety that is listed No.4C 1820;[3] this sovereign (Plate No.4) appeared for the first time in the Stetchworth Cambridgeshire Hoard of 11 August 1980. The hoard consisted of 106 gold coins, all of which were sovereigns and half sovereigns from 1817 to 1825.

Note. I am most grateful to Sotheby's of London for kindly providing the photographs for Plate No. 3.

Description and details of the new sovereign.

Obverse. The king's head right, laureate with short hair; the tie has a loop with two ends, neck bare. Legend GEORGIUS III D:G:BRITANNIAR:REX F:D: The date is shown at the bottom of the coin under truncation.

---

2. Sotheby's, *Coins, Medals and Banknotes*. London 15-16 October 1998. Sale LN 8661 Lot No 286.
3. *Coin Hoards* No VII Royal Numismatic Society 1985 p 372.

5

Reverse. St.George with streamer flowing from helmet, mounted and slaying the Dragon with a spear, the device being placed within the garter which replaces the legend and is inscribed HONI.SOIT.QUI.MAL.Y.PENSE. On the ground under the broken shaft of the spear are the tiny letters B.P. They are shown incuse and of course stand for Benedetto Pistrucci, and just below them cleverly placed on the buckle of the garter are the initials W.W.P. They are incuse and represent the Master, William Wellesley Pole.

The coin is struck with a reverse die axis.

Edge. Milled.

The weight was to be 123.274 grains. The fineness 22 carat 11/12 fine gold 1/12 alloy.

The weight and fineness of the sovereign has not altered, and has remained constant right through to the present day.

Millesimal fineness 916.66

Thickness .067 of an inch

Diameter .868 of an inch

SOVEREIGNS OF GEORGE III

NO.	DATE		MINTAGE	RATING
1.	1817		3,235,239	N
2.	1818		2,347,230	N
2A.	1818	Ascending colon after BRITANNIAR·. clear space between REX and F:D:	inc. with above	S
2B.	1818	Wiry curls, legend as normal	inc. with above	S
2C.	1818	Wiry curls, legend as 2A	inc. with above	R
3.	1819		3,574	R6
4.	1820	Normal date	*2,101,994	S
4A.	1820	Short date figures	inc. with above	R
4B.	1820	Small O in date	inc. with above	R
4C.	1820	First digit in date a letter I	inc. with above	R

* This figure has been increased to 2,101,994 because the dies of 1820 continued to be used for the first year of the reign of George IV.

Plate 2.

Actual Size

Obverse and Reverse of Sovereign No. 1.

Plate 3.

Obverse and Reverse of Sovereign No. 3.

Plate 4.

Obverse and Reverse of Sovereign No. 4C.

GEORGE IV 1820-1830

After the death of George III on 29 January 1820 it was decided that the Mint should continue to use the old dies of George III. So in fact all the sovereigns struck in 1820 bore the bust of George III.

William Wellesley Pole continued as Master of the Mint, and the engraving staff were only Pistrucci and William Wyon. However, Pistrucci appealed strongly to Pole that the engraving staff ought to be brought more up to strength, and recommended the appointment of Jean Baptiste Merlen a Frenchman, and on 11 February 1820 Merlen was made Assistant Engraver to Pistrucci.

During the reign of George IV there were to be two different designs of sovereigns, and the first was authorized by Order in Council dated 5 May 1821 in accordance with the following submission bearing the date 10 April 1821 by William Wellesley Pole, Master of the Mint:

"In further pursuance of your Majesty's Commands that Dies should be prepared for the Coining of Your Majesty's Monies I humbly beg leave to lay before Your Majesty a Design for the Gold Sovereign or Twenty Shilling piece having for the Obverse Impression the effigy of Your Majesty with the Inscription 'Georgius IIII D.G.Britanniar Rex F:D: and for the Reverse the Image of St.George, armed, sitting on horseback attacking the Dragon with a Sword having broken his Spear in the Encounter, and the date of the Year. The edge of the piece is intended to be marked with the new invented Graining used on Coins of His late Majesty."

The new coinage was by now becoming an urgent requirement and Pistrucci began his work, and all the obverses for the entire coinage including the sovereign were modelled and cut by him. He in fact engraved the same laureate head bust that he had used for the Coronation Medal. The sovereign reverse was also modelled and engraved by Pistrucci, featuring a slightly changed version of St.George slaying the Dragon and bearing the date 1821.

The 'laureate head' sovereigns were in fact issued for every year up to and including 1825, and low grade coins for the more common years of 1821, 1822 or 1824 can easily be found. However, a word of caution is necessary in respect of the 1822 date, for counterfeits are to be found. Without doubt there are two very rare dates within the 'laureate head' series, the 1823 and 1825 (Plate No.5), and in the case of the 1825 sovereign I would ask you to note a change in my rarity rating of this coin. Once more it seems the last twenty years have been indicative of my change, and the availability of this coin seems to have become much less. I have no hesitation in elevating the rarity rating of it from R.2 to R.3.

Last year I noted an example of the 1823 sovereign in E.F. condition that sold for £1000. I would stress that any sovereigns with high rarity rating and in really good condition are likely to command very high prices when available. Evidence of this has been clearly shown by the recent sale of the 1819 sovereign I mentioned earlier.

Description and details.

Obverse. The King's bust to the left, laureate, tye with loop at two ends, hair short and bare neck. B.P. in small letters below truncation standing for Benedetto Pistrucci.
Legend GEORGIUS IIII D:G:BRITANNIAR:REX F:D:
Reverse. St.George slaying the Dragon. The date is shown below the exergue line with the letters B.P. to the right for Benedetto Pistrucci.
The coin is struck with a reverse die axis.
Edge. Milled.

Note The streamer is missing from the helmet. There is a difference in the arrangement of the cloak, and this time St.George is armed with a sword.

LAUREATE HEAD SOVEREIGNS OF GEORGE IV

NO.	DATE	VARIETIES	MINTAGE	RATING
5.	1821		9,405,114	N
6.	1822		6,356,787	N
7.	1823		616,770	R3
8.	1824		3,767,904	S
9.	1825		(See 1825 'Bare Head' issue).	R3

Before going into details of the 'new bare head' series that followed, it is necessary to record a chapter of events that occurred during 1823 and 1824. These events were to have a considerable effect on the proposed new coinage. Pole had become upset at a Cabinet reconstruction in 1823 and resigned as Master in the August of that year, and he was replaced by Thomas Wallace in October 1823. Wallace was considered a good replacement, and he was in fact particularly keen on the design of coins.

During 1823 the English sculptor Francis Legatt Chantrey (1781-1841) was asked to prepare a bust of the King, and it was little wonder because the King fancied a new bust and Chantrey was a sculptor of the highest merit. He had studied art at the Royal Academy of which he was elected a member in 1818, and he was knighted by William IV in 1830. He earned the distinction of being the finest bust sculptor of his time. It was inevitable that the King decided to accept the Chantrey bust for the proposed new coinage of 1825, and he also requested that it should be used as model for the effigy on the obverse of the new double-sovereign to be struck in 1823, Pistrucci was then asked to use Chantrey's model and to proceed with the engraving of the new coin, and this he promptly refused to do. Throughout his career this had always been Pistrucci's way of work, and he would only work from life, indeed many including the King had previously accepted Pistrucci's chosen method of work before. He had made it very clear that he felt it degrading to copy another artist's work, but this time the King insisted that the Chantrey bust should be used. The new Master reported that Pistrucci had refused to carry out his orders and as a result he was relieved of his duties, and it was in fact Merlen who eventually engraved the obverse die for the double-sovereign.

On 23 June 1824 the Master of the Mint recommended that Merlen be employed to prepare the design and engrave dies for the new series of gold and silver coins. At the same time William Wyon, the Second Engraver, was called to prepare designs and engrave the head dies for the proposed new coinage. Later, on 15 January 1828, with Pistrucci already having lost his position, William Wyon was given the Chief Engraver's post, and Pistrucci the somewhat lower position of Chief Medallist, though both were given the same salary - £350 a year.

The new 'bare head' sovereign was first issued in 1825 and thus there are two different types of sovereign for this year, and this type was struck until the end of the reign in 1830. (Plate No.6).

The 'bare head' sovereign of this reign will in general present the collector with more problems to add to his collection, and only the year of 1826 can be considered as easy to acquire. Four of the other sovereigns, 1825, 1827, 1829 and 1830 are all rated scarce, and in good grade they will be difficult to find, and perhaps at around £350 to £450 each. Finally I come to 1828, and this year's coin is without doubt the rarest sovereign of the 'bare head' series. It is the low mintage of this coin that causes it to be rated R4, and this is explained because most of the coinage struck for 1828 was from old 1827 dies which were kept in use, it was only near the end of the year when the new 1828 dies were used. A recent example of the 1828 sovereign in V.F. condition was sold for £2300.

Description and details.

Obverse. The King's head to the left bare. Date shown below truncation on field. Inscription reading GEORGIUS IV DEI GRATIA.
Reverse. The Ensigns Armorial of the United Kingdom contained in a beautiful ornate shield surmounted by the royal crown; the centre of the shield features

a smaller shield surmounted by a small crown, and within this shield are displayed the Hanoverian Arms.

Legend reading BRITANNIARUM REX FID: DEF:

The coin is struck with a reverse die axis.

Edge. Milled.

Note. Obverse. William Wyon engraved the King's bust from Chantrey's bust.

   Reverse. Jean Baptiste Merlen designed and engraved the reverse dies

BARE HEAD SOVEREIGNS OF GEORGE IV

NO.	DATE	VARIETIES	MINTAGE	RATING
10.	1825		4,200,343*	S
11.	1826		5,724.046	N
12.	1827		2,266,629	S
13.	1828		386,182	R4
14.	1829		2,444,652	S
15.	1830		2,387.881	S

*   This figure includes the 1825 laureate head mintage.

Before leaving this reign I will tell you of another interesting hoard of sovereigns found quite close to me in the small village of Birdbrook in Essex;[1] it is known as the Birdbrook (Yew Tree Cottage) Essex Hoard 27.7.1977.

The hoard was buried in a metal box under a loose brick floor, and it contained ninety nine gold sovereigns. Fifty nine of these coins were from the reign of George IV and they began at 1825 ending at the date of 1830, but the group failed to produce any rare or new varieties. No sovereigns of William IV were included, and the remaining forty sovereigns were all from the Type 1A series of Victoria, beginning in 1838 and finishing with a single coin dated 1845. The remaining part of the hoard were in E.F. condition, and some very near to uncirculated pieces. (Plate No. 15)[2] This sovereign was from the hoard.

The hoard was of course declared, and I was myself fortunate to assist in the examination of it. Eventually the coins were returned to the finder.

---

1. *Coin Hoards* Volume IV. The Royal Numismatic Society London 1978. No.406 p123.
2. My grateful thanks to Mr.B.Tuck of Ipswich for the loan of the 1843 sovereign to photograph and use in Plate No.15.

Plate 5.

Actual Size

Obverse and Reverse of the 'Laureate Head' Sovereign No. 9.

GEORGE IV

Plate 6.

Actual Size

Obverse and Reverse of the 'Bare Head' Sovereign No. 15.

15

WILLIAM IV 1830-1837

William IV succeeded his brother on 26 June 1830, and for sometime it appeared little or nothing was being done about the new coinage, and on 15 November 1830 the Master of the Mint, John Charles Herries M.P. felt it was necessary to explain why there was a delay in the preparation of the new dies; he said:

"The delay which has occurred in presenting the Memorial since His Majesty's commands were issued although not beyond the usual period, has arisen in consequence of the difficult and anxious desire to obtain an accurate and approved resemblance of his Majesty, who was pleased to command that the effigy on his coins should be taken from the Bust which was executed at the time by Mr.Chantrey."

For this purpose it was desirable that a model should be prepared by Mr.Chantrey adapted to the style used on the Coinage before Mr.Wyon could be set to work; this of course occupied some time in addition to the time required by Mr.Wyon for engraving the Dies on Steel (always a work of much labour) and the more so on this occasion when it was necessary to be done under the immediate personal superintendance and instruction of Mr.Chantry."

Shortly after this statement Herries resigned and in December of that year was replaced by George Eden, 2nd Earl of Auckland, who remained Master until 1834. However, the dies for the new coinage had in fact been prepared before the Herries statement, because on 28 October 1830 the Master had written to the Mint Board as follows:

"Mr.Herries communicates to the Mint Board His Majesty's entire approbation of the Engraving of the Head of His Majesty for the New coin executed by Mr.Wyon, from the model prepared by Mr.Chantrey, to whom His Majesty was graciously pleased to sit for the purpose.

Mr.Herries further acquaints the Board that it is His Majesty's pleasure that Engraving from the same model, and from no other, shall be used for all coins, whether in Gold, Silver or Copper that are to bear the effigys of His Majesty in order that there may be a perfect uniformity throughout the Coinage of His Majesty's Reign in that respect."

The design of the new coinage that included the sovereign was approved by an Order in Council dated 22 November 1830 and according to the following description:

The Sovereign having for the Obverse Impression the Effigy of Your Majesty with the inscription GULIELMUS IIII D.G.BRITANNIAR. REX F.D. and for the reverse the Ensigns Armorial of the United Kingdom contained in a Shield - plain - with the date of the year and a graining on the edge of the piece.

William Wyon, the Chief Engraver, engraved the dies from the model once again prepared by Francis Legatt Chantrey, and the reverse was both designed and engraved by Jean Baptiste Merlen.

Before going on to deal in general with sovereigns of this reign I think it necessary to up-date you with the exciting new discoveries I have established within the reign since 1980; they are not only new varieties but also a new bust type. I am sure readers will remember that I said in the first edition of *The Gold Sovereign* how difficult it was to obtain the sovereigns of William IV; they seldom appear either in low or high grade. It is of course essential if one is to establish new varieties, etc., for a large number of coins to be examined. During the early eighties, thanks to the kindness of collectors, dealers, correspondents, and some auctions I was able to examine quite a few William sovereigns. This enabled me to put together a paper with considerable foundation that I published in the *Spink Numismatic Circular* of May 1984,[1] and in my paper of that year to reveal a new bust type within the series. Since 1984 I have seen a few more William sovereigns and I can say that they further endorse my paper of 1984.

As a result of what I have just said we now have a first and second bust for the series and these are the main features that distinguish the difference between the two busts:

First bust. The bust is in general slightly larger. (Plate No.8)
The nose is larger with nostril more pronounced and points directly at the second N in BRITANNIAR.
The hair arrangement at the top of the forehead is a single curl almost horizontal with a thin strand lying on its top pointed at each end, and there is a small gap between this and a small cluster of four curls that sit on the top of the head.
The hair on the nape of the neck at the bottom turns into the neck and is quite tight on it.
A curl of hair covers most of the top rear edge of the ear.
The initials W.W. incuse and with stops spaced wider than usual.
The legend, on this bust, is generally more clearly spaced.

Second Bust. Nose is smaller and points directly at the letter I next to the last N of BRITANNIAR. (Plate No.8).
The hair arrangement at the top of the forehead is now one single curl, again

---

1. M.A.Marsh, 'William IV Sovereign. A Different Bust and a New Variety', *Spink Numismatic Circular* May 1984, pp118-119.

17

almost horizontal and bending back towards a similar cluster of four curls on the top of the head; a slightly different space separates the two.

The hair above the ear this time allows almost all of the top part of the ear to be seen.

The obverse edge beading is noticeably coarser.

The initials W.W. incuse and with stops are closer together.

The legend is very poorly spaced and with several letters and figures touching each other.

The first type bust was introduced in 1831, and my survey results suggested that the new second bust would have been introduced in 1832. However, I have now seen three sovereigns dated 1832, but with the first bust, so my conclusion is that the 1832 coin with the first bust must be regarded as rare.

Another variety of the first bust type is one that perhaps should have been published in 1980, but I confess that at that time I did not have a copy of Captain K.J.Douglas-Morris R.N. Auction Catalogue of 1974.[1] In fact I only spotted this particular variety in it a year or so later when I obtained my own copy. Lot No.182 is a currency sovereign dated 1831; it is the first bust type and WW on the truncation is without stops. It is described as practically mint state and very rare. I know of only two other examples of this coin; one was sold by Spink & Son Ltd. several years ago, the other is in a local collection (Plate No.7).

The next variety was kindly sent to me by John Duggan of Blackburn to examine, and it is a sovereign bearing the date of 1837 (Plate No.9). It has to be the most unusual error date I have ever seen, and my grateful thanks to Mr.G.P.Dyer and the engraving staff of the Royal Mint who gave me so much assistance with this particular coin.

It seems certain that when the engraver began this amazing series of errors the die included the figures 183 of the date, and I feel the engraver's first mistake occurred because he disliked the 3 that was before him. He decided either to repair or reposition this figure. However, he did neither; in error he punched in the 3 over 8. When he discovered this monumental mistake I think he may well have become so distraught that his next effort became even more disastrous, and the 8 punch he then tried to use over the 3 was entered so low that it almost fouled the border beading. In fact tool marks are clearly visible on one of the beads directly below the 8, and this bead is somewhat reduced in shape and size. It is therefore quite clear that at this point he made some effort to rectify his errors. Finally he made his last desperate effort to correct this catastrophic series of errors; the 8 punch was again used and this time in the

1. Captain K.J.Douglas-Morris R.N., *The Distinguished Collection of English Gold Coins* 1700-1900. Sotheby and Co Catalogue - Nov 1974, Lot No.182.

correct place. However the two 8's can be clearly seen because the first is positioned slightly more to the right than the last entered 8. Both the left and right diagonal parts of the 3 are visible within the top loop of the 8, and the first corner of the same section can be seen emerging from under the 8 on the top right corner of the figure. The horizontal top of the 3 is also visible along the top of the 8, and the inner lower part of the 3 can be clearly seen within the bottom loop of the 8. Finally the large lower half of his first entered 8 is seen very clearly hanging below the full figure 8 of the date.

This particular die was such an atrocious and obvious piece of bad workmanship that it is unlikely to have escaped notice for very long, and then it would have been withdrawn and possibly destroyed. If this were the case I do not think many coins would have been struck from it, and so the variety must be considered as very rare.

The final new variety is in fact a much simpler piece to identify than the error date I have just described, and this sovereign[2] is a second bust type dated 1836. Shown on the reverse side at the bottom, just above the word ANNO, another letter N has been entered into the lower garnishing directly above the last N in ANNO. It is very surprising that when one examines this error it looks as though no attempt has been made to correct it. This sovereign has been examined by Mr.G.P.Dyer of the Royal Mint and he has said to me that the letter N in question may have been deliberately placed, but at this time there is nothing to suggest what the letter N might be attributed to. However, we do of course know of sovereigns that have a special mark for identification purposes, and the best known of these is the 'Ansell' sovereign (M.A.M. 42A), so perhaps time again will provide an answer? Meantime I would always be pleased to hear from any reader who might be able to assist with information, or if perhaps he may have an example of the 1836 'N' sovereign. (Plate No.10). My own firm expectation is that other specimens will turn up and for this reason I have not felt justified in giving it a rarity rating better than R.2.

Description and details.

Obverse. The King's bare head to right. At the base of the truncation the letters W.W. incuse, with stops, standing for William Wyon.
Legend. GULIELMUS IIII D:G:BRITANNIAR: REX F:D:
Reverse. The Ensigns Armorial of the United Kingdom within a shield surmounted by a crown, in the centre a smaller shield containing the Hanoverian Arms, and surmounted by a small crown.

---

2. I first noticed this sovereign on the list of Cheshire dealer Mr Roy Stirling in October 1995 and he kindly referred me to the owner, Mr B Williams of Shetland. I am most grateful to both for their co-operation in respect of this new variety.

The date is shown in the field at the bottom of the right side.
The word ANNO in a similar position on the left side.
The coin is struck with a reverse die axis.
Edge. Milled.

Note. Obverse. William Wyon engraved the King's bust from a model by
Chantrey.
Reverse. Jean Baptiste Merlen designed and engraved the reverse dies.

SOVEREIGNS OF WILLIAM IV

NO.	DATE	VARIETIES	MINTAGE	RATING
16.	1831	First bust. Nose points towards second N of BRITANNIAR; W.W. incuse with stops	598,547	R2
16A.	1831	First bust. WW incuse without stops.	Inc. in above	R5
17.	1832	Second bust. Nose points towards letter I next to last N of BRITANNIAR; W.W. incuse with stops		
17A.	1832	First bust. W.W. incuse with stops.	Inc. in above	S
18.	1833	Second bust.	1,225,269	S
19.	1835	Second bust.	723,441	R
20.	1836	Second bust.	1,714,349	S
20A.	1836	Second bust. Rev. additional letter N above ANNO.	Inc. in above	R2
21.	1837	Second bust.	1,172,984	S
21A.	1837	Second bust. Rev.Error date 8	inc. in above	R3

Note. More details of busts and varieties are on pages 17 and 18.

WILLIAM IV

Plate 7.

Actual Size

Obverse and Reverse of the First bust Sovereign No. 16A. WW (No stops)

Plate 8.

Obverse of First bust Sovereign No. 16A.

Obverse of Second bust Sovereign No. 21A.

Plate 9.

Obverse and Reverse of Sovereign No. 21A. (Error date)

Plate 10.

Obverse and Reverse of Sovereign No. 20A.

Enlarged 'ANNO' area of Reverse Sovereign No. 20A.

VICTORIA 1837-1901

Queen Victoria began her reign upon the death of her uncle on 20 June 1837. The first important change necessary was that of the royal arms, because they included the Hanoverian Arms. The right to the Kingdom of Hanover was limited only to the male line, and they had been included in the royal arms since the accession to the throne of George I. The change was in fact effected by an Order in Council dated 26 July 1837 which provided for the Arms of Hanover to be omitted.

On 22 August 1837 the Chancellor of the Exchequer wrote to [1]Henry Labouchere, 1st Baron Taunton, who was Master of the Mint as follows:

"Her Majesty has commanded me to direct that the Chief Engraver and the Medallist of Her Majesty's Mint shall attend at Windsor Castle on Friday next for the purpose of having the advantage of study for their models in their respective departments.

They should be at Windsor very early and should report their arrival to the Lord or Groom in waiting.

Her Majesty will give the artists separate sittings on Friday."

William Wyon, the Chief Engraver attended at Windsor and prepared a wax model of the Queen's bust. It was interesting to note that Pistrucci although Medallist at that time did not attend, and it is very likely that Jean Baptiste Merlen was involved with the reverse design. He certainly carried out the engraving. The new bust of the Queen that is known as the 'Young head' is a fine example of design and engraving by William Wyon, and the bust of the Queen is shown turned to the left, head bound with a double fillet, and the hair gracefully gathered up into a knot behind.

The designs for the sovereign were submitted to the Queen by Labouchere on 15 February 1838 as follows:

"In pursuance of Your Majesty's gracious Command that Dies for your Majesty's Coins should be prepared according to the Model of an Effigy of your Majesty, which I had the honour to submit for Your Majesty's approbation, and also new reverses for the Gold and Silver Coinage.

I humbly beg leave to lay before your Majesty the annexed specimen of the Impression intended to be struck on the Sovereign or twenty shilling piece namely for the Obverse Impression the aforesaid Effigy of your Majesty with the inscription 'Victoria Dei Gratia' and the date of the Year. For the Reverse Impression the Ensigns Armorial of the United Kingdom according to the Design approved by Your Majesty in Council dated 26 July 1837 contained in a plain shield, surmounted by the Royal Crown and encircled with a Laurel Wreath, with the inscription Britanniarum Regina Fid:Def: having the united

---

1. Sir John Craig K.C.V.O., C.B., L.L.D. *The Mint* Cambridge 1953, pp 301-314

Rose, Thistle and Shamrock placed under the Shield." The design of the obverse was engraved by William Wyon and the reverse by Jean Baptiste Merlen, and they were approved on 26 February 1838.

The first of the 'shield' Type 1A sovereigns issued bore the date of 1838 (Plate No.22) and so began what was to be another most interesting period in the history of our gold coinage.

During this first period of Victoria's coinage there were most important changes in the Mint; in 1841 Henry Labouchere, the Master, resigned and was replaced by William Ewart Gladstone M.P., who later became Prime Minister. Gladstone took much interest in his appointment, especially in the recoinage, and in his four-year spell as Master he made a valuable contribution to the running and efficiency of the Mint. He resigned in February 1845.

In July 1844 Jean Baptiste Merlen retired at the age of 75; he had been a member of the engraving staff since February 1820 when he was appointed Assistant to Pistrucci. So finally the Frenchman ended a long and valuable period of service to the Mint, and Leonard Charles Wyon, the son of William, was appointed Second Engraver to his father on 23 July 1844.

A new Master was appointed in 1845: and it was Sir George Clerk M.P. who was Secretary of the Treasury, but he only held the post for a year. In July 1846 he was succeeded by Richard Lalor Shiel M.P. who continued as Master until December 1850, during which time he took a very active part in the running of the Mint and was instrumental in some important changes near the end of his time. Sir John Frederick William Herschel, Fellow and former Secretary of the Royal Society, was appointed the new Master in 1851, and it was at this time that other important things were happening in places far away from England that would have considerable effect on our gold coinage.

It was in May 1851 that gold was discovered in Australia, first in New South Wales and shortly afterwards in Victoria, and this led to heavy demands being made on the currency coinage of the colonies. These demands could not be met, and a petition by the Council of New South Wales was addressed to Her Majesty on 19 December 1851. It asked for a branch of the Royal Mint to be established at Sydney so that the people could convert their gold into money.

In South Australia the Adelaide Chamber of Commerce tried to help matters by acquiring in 1852 an Assay Office for assaying gold ingots, but they exceeded their powers by striking the Adelaide Token, or Pound as it became known. However, it was not to last long and the office was closed by Proclamation on 17 February 1853.

By Order of Council dated 19 August 1853 a branch mint for Sydney was authorized and it opened on 14 May 1855.[2] The second branch mint at Melbourne opened on 12 June 1872.

---

2. Sir Geoffrey Duveen and H.G.Stride, *The History of The Gold Sovereign*. London 1962, p95.

An act passed in 1863 which, after stating that Queen Victoria had by Proclamation established the Sydney branch mint for making gold coins, the same as those issued by the Royal Mint in London, said it would be lawful for the Queen by Proclamation, and with the advice of her Privy Council, to declare that after a date given in the Proclamation gold coins made at the branch mint of designs approved by Her Majesty, and that they should be of the same fineness and weight, etc. as those struck at the Royal Mint, London. They would then be legal tender within the United Kingdom of Britain and Ireland.

In 1866 the Colonial Branch Mint Act was passed. This gave a general power to the Queen, again by Proclamation, and so because of these two Acts the coins struck at the branch mints would be legal tender. However, the first series of Australian sovereigns struck at the Sydney branch mint in 1855 were not accepted as currency outside New South Wales; there had been problems over the design of these sovereigns, and also relating to their light colour caused by the use of silver as an alloy, instead of copper, to form an alloy of the prescribed legal standard. They were in fact only recognised as legal tender sovereigns in the United Kingdom after 1866. So the Australian sovereign was first struck at the Sydney branch mint in 1855 and 1856, and the design of the first issue featured the bust of Victoria to the left, a very similar bust to the Type 1A Shield sovereign, but certainly not of the same standard. The date appears below, and the legend surrounds the bust. The reverse of the coin is very different; it has AUSTRALIA across the centre of the field with a branch of oak leaves on either side and the words, ONE SOVEREIGN at the bottom of the coin. SYDNEY MINT is placed in a similar way at the top. The sovereign became known as the 'filleted head'.

In 1851 James Wyon, a cousin of L.C.Wyon, was appointed resident engraver at the Royal Mint, and it was he who engraved the first Australian Sydney branch mint sovereign. However, it failed to meet with approval and was replaced with a new bust and a wreath of native Banksia; a slight change was made in the legend, but otherwise the coin is similar to the first issue. This new second bust is by L.C.Wyon and continues through until the series finished in 1870. Incidentally all die work for the Australian branch mints was done in London by the current engraver of the Mint, and then sent by ship to Australia. The branch mints did not have engraving staff, but some date alterations were made at the Melbourne branch mint which I will describe later.

The new Sydney sovereign met with a certain amount of success when it was first issued and several countries adopted it as legal tender. However, one country, India, found it more useful as a bullion coin, and bearing in mind the circumstances of India at that time, when there was a suggestion of the introduction of a 10 Rupee gold piece as legal tender, then I am sure the United Kingdom would have seen the Australian sovereign as a more suitable alternative. [1]Indeed Col. J.T.Smith F.R.S. late Master of the Fort St.George and Calcutta Mints was as ever fully aware of the Indian situation; he was indeed most able, and often kept London well informed.

Sovereigns from the shield series of Type 1A, 1B, 1C and 1D are, I feel, the most attractive of Victoria's reign; they will present the collector with a great deal of difficulty especially if he wants to acquire them in top condition; even many coins rated as common or normal will still fall into this category. There are two important factors that contribute greatly to the difficulty I have mentioned, and one is that during Victoria's reign the sovereign was used very much for trading purposes, and being made of such soft gold, it took only a short period of time for wear to become very evident. The other big factor was the very large recoinage that took place between 1842 and 1845 when more than £14,000,000 of light gold was withdrawn; this was estimated to be one third of the total gold in circulation. Something like £500,000 more per year of below legal limit gold continued to be taken out of circulation after 1845.

Shortly after *The Gold Sovereign* was published in 1980 I managed, after many years of patient searching,[2] to find a sovereign that I always believed could exist. This was an overdate from the sovereign series of the London Mint, and it was a variety that had never before been recorded and one indeed that many felt could not exist.

My patience was rewarded when I discovered the sovereign bearing the date of 1843 with the 3 in fact over a 2. (M.A.M.26B) (Plate No.12). I was very fortunate to be able to examine the sovereign under the Electron Scanning Microscope, and also to have the benefit of its wonderful stereonic photographs (Plate No.13). This was the first time the Scanning Microscope had been used for numismatic purposes, and it proved conclusively that at long last an overdate from the London Mint sovereign series had been established. The 1843/2 overdate is certainly a key date within the series, and extremely rare, a fact I am sure greatly enhanced by the recoinage of 1842-1845.

I move now to a most important Auction of mainly gold sovereigns that for the collector and students alike presented a wonderful opportunity, and I refer to the Douro Cargo.[3] This cargo of some 28,000 gold coins, mainly consisting of sovereigns, was recovered from the R.M.S.Douro that sank in the Bay of Biscay in 1882. The cargo included sovereigns of Victoria from 1838 to 1881, and 10,000 were catalogued as collectable coins, of which around forty of these were key dates and major rarities. However, before going into these I have to say that even a cargo of such a huge quantity as this could not

---

1. Col J.T.Smith F.R.S. *Remarks on a Gold Currency for India and Proposal of Measures for the Introduction of the British Sovereign.* London 1868.
2. M.A.Marsh. *Seaby Coin & Medal Bulletin.* December 1981. pp348-349.
3. Spink and Son Ltd. *The Douro Cargo.* London, St James's 20 and 21 November 1996 Auction No 118.

quite yield all of the extremely rare sovereigns within the reign of Victoria; two were missing. One was the major rarity of the Type 11A series the 1879 sovereign (M.A.M.90) (Plate No.26), and the other missing sovereign was the 1843/2 overdate from the Type 1A series (M.A.M.26B), another major rarity and key date. Amongst the very rare group of sovereigns from the cargo were two varieties of 1863 '827' sovereigns (M.A.M.46A), the other being from the die number series, and a significant point is that they were the only two '827' sovereigns from the cargo, and so further endorse the rarity rating which I believe they fully deserve. The die number coin realized £2530, and the other variety fetched £3080, and both sovereigns were described as 'bold V.F.', these were figures in the region of what I expected. Another very rare sovereign was the 1843 (narrow shield) variety (M.A.M.26A) which was described as V.F. except for an obverse edge knock, and it realized £2640. Few of these sovereigns are known to exist and I have seen only one (Plate No.14); I have always thought it to be either a proof or pattern piece. However, I felt it must be included. The Douro coin, conditionwise, does suggest it may well have been in circulation so there is certainly room for further thought on this particular variety. There were thirteen of the rare key date 'Ansell' sovereigns (M.A.M.42A) but only two of these were good grade coins; both were EF/GEF, one fetched £1320 and the other £880. The other examples were all around V.F., and this again I felt endorses a view I have always held. This rare key date does occasionally turn up but hardly ever above V.F. The other really rare coin from the TYPE 1B die number series is the 1874 date (M.A.M.58), and seven of these surfaced. All except one piece bore the die number 32, which is that usually seen when this very rare sovereign appears. The highest graded coin of these six was described as A.E.F.; it realized £2090. The remaining sovereign bore the so far unrecorded die number of 33; it was graded G.V.F. and fetched £3300. Finally we had from the Douro three sovereigns bearing the date 1841 (M.A.M.24), and these extremely rare key date coins were all of variable V.F. grades. The best coin of the trio was graded V.F./G.V.F. and realized £902.

I have so far written quite a lot regarding the varieties and types within the Young head/shield sovereign coinage of Victoria, and before I go on I feel it necessary to draw your attention back to the first edition of *The Gold Sovereign* published in 1980, and on page 22 I was able to define in three separate groups the different sovereigns that I knew existed within the Types 1A and 1B series. I finished with the following paragraph that I feel is still accurate:

'Some of the varieties I have mentioned, I am sure were never intended to be definite varieties. I am certain they occurred only as a result of the touching up of the various dies - a process that was common to the engraver of that time. Whether they are definite varieties or not, I feel that they must be mentioned in this book because they do genuinely exist.'

For several years there has always been considerable conjecture surrounding the early sovereigns of Victoria, especially those within the Type 1A series, but I do not wish to change the view I have held since 1980. However, other variations have been noted since, and it is only right that, as you will see, they are included in this edition. I also include the three main groups again of 1, 2 and 3 that break down the series in the best definable way (Plate No.22). To conclude on this somewhat questionable series perhaps I can do no better than quote the words of [1]William Wyon himself when addressing the Royal Commission on the Mint in 1848:

"With respect to the dies every die is perfected by the Graver, re-lettered etc., and in fact made an original before it is hardened; so that, in case of a failure of the original matrix, a die could be converted into and used as a matrix, so as to obtain puncheons from it."

I cannot conclude the Young head series without describing in detail one of the key coins from the Type 1A series, the 'Ansell' sovereign (M.A.M.42A), and it is so named because of the remarkable efforts of George Frederick Ansell who was employed by the Royal Mint. [2]Thomas Graham F.R.S. became Master of the Mint in 1856 and on 29 October that year he wrote to the Treasury recommending the appointment of Ansell; in accordance with this recommendation to a supernumerary clerkship, he took office in the Rolling Room of the Royal Mint. Graham had described him as 'a person of superior education and ability, and great activity and vigour of character'. He also had a very significant scientific background.[3] In 1859 a quantity of gold valued at £167,539 was ordered to be melted and returned to the Bank as unfit for coin due to its brittle nature; this gold in fact contained small quantities of antimony, arsenic and lead. Ansell asked to experiment with this gold, and although confronted by several obstacles, including the aversion to change, he was eventually given permission. His experiments brought a successful conclusion and as a result all of the gold was re-wrought at very little additional cost, and without annealing. The new sovereigns were in fact so tough that an ordinary man could not break them even with the aid of a pair of pliers. For his efforts Ansell received a letter of thanks from the Master of the Mint plus £100.

The 'Ansell' sovereign can be recognised by a small additional line that Ansell had placed in the centre lower edge of the ribbon at the back of Victoria's head (Plate No.16). I discovered two new varieties in 1981 and in fact published both in 1982. Both are of course now included, and the first of these is an 1861 sovereign listed (M.A.M.44A) that has the first digit of its date shown as a letter I. I know of only one other example of this coin, and it appeared in the

---

1. Sir Geoffrey Duveen and H.G.Stride. *The History of The Gold Sovereign*. London 1962 p.86.
2. G.F. Ansell. *The Royal Mint* Third edition. London 1871. pp49-52.
3. M.A.Marsh The Ansell Sovereign. *Spink Numismatic Circular* July 1982 pp 194-195.

'Douro' cargo. The second new variety you will note is listed (M.A.M.45A), and this sovereign dated 1862 features on the reverse an F over inverted A over F in DEF: I think both sovereigns are very rare. (Plates No.17, 18). Another rare and interesting error date sovereign was sent to me by an American correspondent, it is dated 1844 and the first 4 is over an inverted 4 (M.A.M.27A) (Plate No.18).

Description and details.

Obverse. Young head of Victoria to left. Hair bound with double fillet and collected up into a knot behind.
Legend VICTORIA DEI GRATIA.
Date on field below truncation. The letters W.W. in relief of the bottom of the truncation at the rear.
These letters also appear incuse on some coins.
Reverse. The Ensigns Armorial within a plain shield and surmounted by a crown. A branch of laurel is shown on each side of the shield. At the bottom the Thistle, Rose and Shamrock are placed with a small flower stop each side.
Legend BRITANNIARUM REGINA FID:DEF:
The coin is struck with a reverse die axis.
Edge. Milled.

TYPE IA SHIELD SOVEREIGNS OF VICTORIA

NO.	DATE	VARIETIES	MINTAGE	RATING
22.	1838		2,718,694	R
22A.	1838	Obv.Type1.Rev.Narrow Shield Different arrangement of laurel with points nearer to crown. The rose, shamrock and thistle are as 26A but with flower stops.	Not known	R3
23.	1839		503,695	R2
24.	1841		124,054	R3
25.	1842		4,865,375	N
26.	1843		5,981,968	N
26A.	1843	Rev.Narrow Shield. Different arrangement of laurel with points nearer to crown. The rose, shamrock and thistle below are larger and better presented but they are without flower stops.	Not known	R4

Type 1A Shield Sovereigns of Victoria - contd.

NO.	DATE	VARIETIES	MINTAGE	RATING
26B.	1843/2	Obv.overdate 3 over 2	Not known	R5
27.	1844		3,000,445	S
27A.	1844	Obv.Error date. 4 next to 8 over inverted 4		R2
28.	1845		3,800,845	S
29.	1846		3,802,947	S
30.	1847		4,667,126	N
31.	1848		2,246,701	S
31A.	1848	Obv.Small head. Group 1	Inc. in above	R2
32.	1849		1,755,399	R
33.	1850		1,402,039	R
34.	1851		4,013,624	N
35.	1852		8,053,435	C
36.	1853		10,597,993	C
37.	1854		3,589,611	N
38.	1855		8,448,482	C
39.	1856		4,806,160	N
40.	1857		4,495,748	N
41.	1858		803,234	R
42.	1859		1,547,603	R
42A.	1859	'Ansell'.(brittle gold)	167,539	R4
43.	1860		2,555,958	S
44.	1861		7,624,736	C
44A.	1861	Obv.First digit in date is a letter I.	Inc. in above	R2
45.	1862		7,836,413	C
45A.	1862	Rev.F over inverted A over F in DEF	Inc. in above	R2
46.	1863		See Type 1B No.48	C
46A.	1863	'827' (Figures on truncation)	Not known	R6
47.	1872		See type 1B No.56	C

We now enter into the Type IB die number series to describe in detail the most important sovereigns within that group; one of these varieties also appears in the Type 1A group (M.A.M.46A) but without die number, and it is known as the '827' sovereign. (Plate Nos.19 and 20 are of (M.A.M.48A) die number variety). This extremely rare sovereign I believe was first found in the hoard of coins discovered at Hatton, Derbyshire, on 6 October 1854 by Mr.E.H.Pugh. The coin bears the date 1863 and carries the die number 22 on the reverse; to date no other die number for this variety has appeared and on all known examples of this sovereign the second 2 of the die number is weakly struck. It is the obverse of the coin which makes it something very special, for at the bottom of the truncation, where one would expect to see the letters W.W. incuse, there are instead the figures 827 in relief.

To what does 827 relate? I said in 1980 that it would not be unreasonable to suggest that 827 in fact related to an ingot number, and past Mint records indicated that experiments were carried out in 1863 involving ingots numbered 816 and 830. However, to establish at least good foundation for the ingot theory, a great deal of searching through existing Royal Mint files and records was necessary.[1] This research was carried out by Mr.G.P.Dyer, Librarian and Curator of the Royal Mint, and full details of this most important research were published by Mr.Dyer in 1977. There cannot be any doubt that the two different varieties of the '827' sovereign are very important key dates within the Young head series, and the Type IA coin without die number is slightly the rarer of the two. Only six of these are so far known, and just nine are recorded for the die number example.

The second and also extremely rare sovereign from this series bears the date 1874 (M.A.M.58) and the 'Douro Cargo' this time produced for us a new die number of 33. This was the first new number for 1874 that I can recall in a long time, and when this sovereign does appear it is invariably with the die number 32.

Description and details.

As the first issue shield except for the die number that is placed on the reverse at the bottom of the coin just above the rose.
The coin is struck with a reverse die axis.

TYPE IB (DIE NUMBER) SHIELD SOVEREIGN OF VICTORIA

NO.	DATE	VARIETIES	MINTAGE	RATING
48.	1863		5,921,669*	N
48A.	1863	827 (Figures on truncation)	Not known	R5
49.	1864		8,656,353	C
50.	1865		1,450,238	S

1. G.P.Dyer. '1863 Sovereign Number 827'. *Spink Numismatic Circular* October 1977, p421.

Type 1B (die number) Shield Sovereign of Victoria - contd.

NO.	DATE	VARIETIES	MINTAGE	RATING
51.	1866		4,047,288	C
52.	1868		1,653,384	N
53.	1869		6,441,322	C
54.	1870		2,189,960	N
55.	1871		8,767,250	C
56.	1872		13,486,708*	C
57.	1873		2,368,215	N
58.	1874		520,713	R4

* These mintage figures include those of the Type IA sovereign of the same date.

There is one final important point I want to emphasize before leaving the Type IB series of die numbers. (Plate No.21)

In the past theories have been advanced to me on the meaning of the die number; probably the best known of these theories is the one that suggests that the number was to produce a record of how many sovereigns that die produced. Well I have never really subscribed to this view, and I am quite certain they were introduced to enable the Mint to pinpoint the coin press operator in respect of that particular die.

You will see when looking through the listings of die numbers that many new die numbers have been added since 1980, and that some of the gaps filled have been of considerable interest. However, without doubt others will appear as more years pass by.

DIE NUMBERS SO FAR KNOWN

1863. 1,2,3,4,5,6,7,8,9,10,11,12,13,14,15,16,17,18,19,20,21,22,23,24,25,26,38

1864. 1,2,3,4,5,6,7,8,9,10,11,12,14,15,16,17,18,20,21,22,23,24,25,26,27,28, 29,30,31,32,33,34,35,36,37,38,39,40,41,42,43,44,45,46,47,48,49,50, 51,52,53,54,55,56,57,58,59,60,61,62,63,64,65,66,68,69,70,71,72,74,75, 76,78,79,80,81,82,83,84,85,86,87,88,89,90,91,92,93,95,96,97,98, 99,100,101,102,103,104,105,106

1865. 1,2,3,4,5,6,7,8,9,10,11,12,13,14,15,16,17,18,19,20,21,22,23,24,25,26, 27,28,29,30,31,32,33,34,35,36,37,38,39,40,41,42,44,51

1866. 1,2,3,4,5,6,7,8,9,10,11,12,13,14,15,16,17,18,19,20,21,22,23,24,25,
26,27,28,29,30,31,32,33,34,35,36,37,38,39,40,41,42,43,45,46,47,
48,49,50,51,52,53,54,55,56,57,58,59,60,61,62,63,64,65,66,68,69,70,
71,72,73,74,75,76,77,78,79

1868. 1,2,3,4,5,6,7,8,9,11,12,13,14,15,16,17,18,19,20,21,22,23,24,25,
26,27,28,29,30,31,32,33,34,35,36,37,38,39,40,41,47,48

1869. 1,2,3,4,5,6,7,8,9,10,11,12,13,14,15,16,17,18,19,20,21,22,23,24,25,
26,27,28,29,30,31,32,33,34,35,36,37,38,39,40,41,42,43,44,45,46,47,
48,49,50,51,52,53,54,55,56,57,58,59,60,61,62,64,65,66,67,68,69,70,71,
72,73,74,75,76

1870. 1,2,3,4,5,6,7,8,9,10,11,12,13,14,15,16,17,18,19,20,21,22,23,24,25,
26,27,28,29,30,31,32,33,34,35,36,37,38,39,40,41,42,43,44,45,46,47,
48,49,50,51,52,53,54,55,56,57,58,59,60,61,62,63,64,65,66,67,68,69,
70,71,72,73,74,75,76,77,78,79,80,81,82,83,84,85,86,87,88,89,90,91,
92,93,94,95,96,99,100,112,113,114,115,116,117,118,119,120,121,
122,123

1871. 1,2,3,4,5,6,7,8,9,10,11,12,13,14,15,16,17,18,19,20,21,22,23,24,25,
26,27,28,29,30,31,32,33,34,35,36,37,38,39,40,41,43,44,45,46,47,48,
49,50,51,52,53,54,55,56,57,58,59,60,61,62,63,64,65,66,67,68,69,
70,71,72,73,74,75,76,77,78,79,83,88,94,96,97,98,99,100,101,
102,103,104,105,106,107, 108,109,110,111

1872. 1,2,3,4,5,6,7,8,9,10,11,12,13,14,15,16,17,18,19,20,21,22,23,24,25,
26,27,28,29,30,31,32,33,34,35,36,37,38,39,40,41,43,44,45,46,47,48,49,
50,51,52,53,54,55,56,57,58,59,60,61,62,63,64,65,67,68,69,70,71,72,73,
74,75,76,77,78,79,80,81,82,83,84,85,86,87,88,89,90,91,92,93,94,95,
96,97,98,99,100,101,102,103,104,105,106,108,109,110,111,112

1873 1,2,3,4,5,6,7,8,9,10,11,12,13,14,15,16,17,18,19,20,21,22,23,24,25,
26,27,28,29,30,31,32,33,34,36,37,38,39,40,41,42,43,44,45,46,47,48,49,
50,51,52,53,54,55,56,57,58,59,60,61,62,63,64,65,66,67,68,69,70,71,
72,73,74,75,76,77,78,79,80,81,82,83,84,85,86,87,88,89,90,91,92,93,94,
95,96,97,98,99,100,103,104,107

1874. 12,15,28,32,33,34,35

Groups within the Type IA and IB Young head/shield series

1. Sovereigns dated 1838 to 1847 inclusive. When the obverse of these coins
    is studied closely it is noticeable that the Queen's head is slightly smaller
    and is well placed in respect of the legend. It does not appear at all cramped

and the letters W.W. are in relief and with stops. The reverse, although containing far more, again displays the legend quite free of the design.

2. Sovereigns dated 1848 to 1855 inclusive. The borders of these coins are slightly broader; because of this the legend of the obverse is moved a little inwards. On the reverse the legend is again forced inwards and is also slightly raised. This gives a very cramped impression of both the laurel branch and legend, and if one looks at the letters T and A in BRITANNIARUM the laurel leaf does in fact encroach between the two letters. Sovereigns dated 1853, 1854 and 1855 within this group can also be found with WW incuse and without stops.

3. Sovereigns dated 1853 to 1871 inclusive. The obverse is similar to that of group 2 coins and the letters WW are incuse and without stops. Sovereigns dated 1870, 1871 and 1872 can be found with W.W. in relief and stops. The remaining sovereigns of the Type IB are with W.W. in relief and with stops.

Note: See Plate No.22 of groups No.1, 2 and 3.

The Melbourne Type IC and the Sydney Type ID shield sovereigns from the branch mints are the same design as the Type IA sovereign, but they can be identified by the mint mark, an M or S that is placed on the reverse at the bottom of the coin just above the rose. (Plate No.23) and (Plate No.24).

These two branch mints do add a great deal of interest for the collector and the more challenging sovereigns are to be found within the Melbourne series. They will present the collector with more than a few problems; those dated 1887, 1886, 1883, 1880 and the 1872/1 overdate are all extremely rare sovereigns, and they are likely to prove quite expensive. It is interesting to note that a G.E.F. example of the 1880 sovereign (M.A.M.61) realized £3740 in the 'Douro' auction.

I think that the most intriguing sovereign from the Melbourne series has to be the 1872/1 overdate (M.A.M.59A) and it certainly deserves to be described as a remarkable coin,[1] I use this expression simply because the branch mints of neither Sydney nor Melbourne were equipped with engraving staff, indeed they had no need of such staff because all die work for their coins was carried out at the London Mint.

Col.E.W.Ward, R.E., who later became Major-General Sir Edward Wohlstenholm Ward, K.C.M.G., R.E., was the Deputy Master of the Melbourne branch mint. Col.Ward had previously been Deputy Master at the Sydney branch mint, and he anticipated that the new Melbourne branch would be ready to open in 1870. This failed to happen and London only supplied dies dated 1871.

---

1. M.A.Marsh, 'Rare Victorian Sovereigns' *Coin Monthly* February 1982, pp6-11.
   M.A.Marsh, 'A Sovereign Overdate from the Melbourne Mint' *Coin Monthly* December 1982, pp 5-7.

The first consignment of these, 100 dies, were sent by the S.S.POONAH from Southampton on 30 September.[1] The POONAH was scheduled to make other calls before eventually transferring her package of dies to the Peninsular and Oriental steamer RANGOON in Galle Harbour, Ceylon on 1 November 1871. The existing Melbourne 1872/1 overdate sovereign (M.A.M.59A) is evidence that at least some of the 1871 dies arrived in Melbourne, though the RANGOON tragically came to grief on the dangerous Cadda rocks shortly after leaving Galle Harbour that evening.

The account reporting the loss of the RANGOON appears in Lloyds List of 23 November 1871 column 23 and states:

"Galle 1st.Nov. The Peninsular and Oriental Company's steamer RANGOON, with mails and passengers for Australia, has struck upon a rock, and is sinking: the passengers have been saved, and the BARODA and two Trinity steamers are saving the mails.

2nd.Nov., 3.a.m. - The RANGOON struck on Cadda rock at 6 last evening, in leaving harbour, and sunk at midnight in 15 fathoms; pilot in charge; passengers, crew, a few bags of mails, and a portion of baggage saved".

The report also states that "The RANGOON would have had on board the cargo which was shipped at Southampton, per POONAH, 30th Sept."

However, new dies for 1872 arrived from London 10 April and 9 May 1872, and these were in time for the planned opening of the Melbourne branch mint 12 June 1872. Again all failed to go according to plan because the dies sent from London failed to produce the number of sovereigns anticipated, in fact the obverse dies only averaged 8000 pieces, and the reverse dies 14000. [2]London believed that this was because the dies were not placed correctly in the presses, but by September the die situation was critical and a local engraver Julius Hogarth was employed. This resulted in some of the 1871 dies being altered by Hogarth, and an example of one of these alterations is in the collection of the Museum of Victoria. Another shown on Plate No.25 (M.A.M.59A) was the first of the temporary engraver's work that I myself came by. It seems certain that Hogarth's work began towards the end of September, and that he only continued for a few weeks until the new dies arrived at the end of October, so one can reasonably suggest that few examples of his unsuccessful work can exist.

I feel the new branch mint overdate (M.A.M.59A) must be regarded as the most unusual overdate of those we know, and so it is without doubt an extremely rare sovereign, and also a key date of the series.

The Type ID Sydney shield sovereigns do not have any coins within the series that can be considered rare, but once again the collector can expect to

---

1. Lloyd's Lists. 23 November 1871 column 23. Libraries and Guildhall Art Gallery, London 1999.
2. J.Sharples, 'The Story of the 1871/1 Sovereign'. *Australian Coin Review*, December 1985

find most of the sovereigns within this series very expensive in top grade.

Before leaving the Melbourne and Sydney branch mints I must refer to three other sovereigns from them that I have seen in other publications during the last year or so, I refer to the 1873 and 1879 coins from the Type 1C Melbourne series of shield sovereigns, and one dated 1877 from the Type IIC St.George series. I have made enquiries regarding these coins in both Australia and England, and I am assured by the Royal Mint that no dies were supplied for any of the three sovereigns in question, so it is difficult to believe that any can exist.

Description and details of the Melbourne and Sydney 'shield' sovereigns:

Type IC and ID.
Obverse. As Type IA. Shield.
Reverse. As Type IA Shield except that the mint mark M or S is placed just above the rose at the bottom of the coin.
The coins are struck with a reverse die axis.
Edge. Milled.

TYPE IC SHIELD SOVEREIGNS OF VICTORIA
(MELBOURNE MINT: MINT MARK M)

NO.	DATE	VARIETIES	MINTAGE	RATING
59.	1872		748,180*	R
59A.	1872/1	Obv.Overdate 2 over 1	Not known	R4
60.	1874		1,373,298	N
61.	1880		3,053,454	R2
62.	1881		2,324,800	R
63.	1882		2,465,781	S
64.	1883		427,450	R2
65.	1884		2,942,630	N
66.	1885		2,967,143	N
67.	1886		2,902,131	R3
68.	1887		1,916,424	R3

*The mintage figure include those of Type IIB sovereigns of the same date.

TYPE ID SHIELD SOVEREIGNS OF VICTORIA
(SYDNEY MINT: MINT MARK S)

NO.	DATE	VARIETIES	MINTAGE	RATING
69.	1871		2,814,000	C
70.	1872		1,815,000	N
71.	1873		1,478,000	S
72.	1875		2,122,000	C
73.	1877		1,590,000	N
74.	1878		1,259,000	S
75.	1879		1,366,000	N
76.	1880		1,459,000	N
77.	1881		1,360,000	S
78.	1882		1,298,000	N
79.	1883		1,108,000	S
80.	1884		1,595,000	N
81.	1885		1,486,000	S
82.	1886		1,667,000	S
83.	1887		1,000,000	S

Charles Fremantle became Deputy Master in 1868 and during his period of office until 1894 he was very much involved in the re-organisation of the Mint. He later became the Hon.Sir Charles Fremantle, K.C.B. In 1871 following Fremantle's efforts a new design for the sovereign was suggested and accepted by the Queen, and was authorized by Order in Council on 14 January 1871. Although William Wyon had died in 1851 his Young head bust of the Queen was kept for the new sovereign. The new reverse was to be the return of Pistrucci's St.George slaying the dragon, the design was the same as that used for the first sovereign of George IV.

The new Type II St.George sovereigns of Victoria were first issued in 1871 and struck at the Royal Mint; during the years 1871 to 1874 they ran concurrently with the 'shield' sovereign. They were also struck at the Melbourne and Sydney branch mints until 1887, and the series is known as the Type II St.George type.

The key date and major rarity from within the whole series of Type II sovereigns, including the branch mints, is unquestionably the 1879 sovereign from the London Mint (M.A.M.90). This sovereign of which only 20,013 were struck is very worthy of an R4 rating; it seldom appears, and even when it does it will be in low grade. In close on forty years I have only once seen a top grade example (Plate No.26). In this condition it must be looked upon in the highest rarity terms.

Most of the other sovereigns from the Type II series in average grade will not present too many problems for the collector, but high grade examples, especially from the branch mints, are likely to prove more expensive and may well cost around the four figure area.

The mint mark for the Type II St.George series of Melbourne and Sydney sovereigns, a letter M or S, is placed on the obverse just below the truncation. (Plates 27 and 28). (Plate No.29) is the Melbourne variety of 103B without B.P.

The second overdate from the London Mint 1880/70 (M.A.M.91A) although more recently discovered can only be rated as scarce, as I have seen quite a few examples. (Plates No.31 and 32).

Description and details.

Obverse. The Queen's head to left. Hair bound with a double fillet and collected up into a knot behind.
Legend. VICTORIA D:G:BRITANNIAR:REG:F:D:* The letters WW incuse at the bottom of the truncation standing for William Wyon.
Reverse. St.George mounted with sword attacking the dragon. The date appears below the exergue line at the bottom with the small letters B.P. to the right. The coin is struck with a reverse die axis.
Edge. Milled.

* It should be noted that on most of these sovereigns the bottom of the truncation is very narrow, consequently the initials WW are often seen encroaching down on to the field area with invariably part of them missing.

TYPE IIA ST.GEORGE SOVEREIGNS OF VICTORIA
VICTORIA (LONDON MINT NO MINT MARK)

NO.	DATE	VARIETIES	MINTAGE	RATING
84.	1871		The figures	C
84A.	1871	Large B.P.	given for these	S
85.	1872		dates of Type IB	C
86.	1873		sovereigns are total	S
87.	1874		figures and include	R
			those sovereigns of	
			Type IIA.	
88.	1876		3,318,866	C

Type IIA St.George Sovereigns of Victoria - contd.

NO.	DATE	VARIETIES	MINTAGE	RATING
89.	1878		1,091,275	N
90.	1879		20,013	R4
91.	1880		3,650,080	C
91A.	1880/70	Rev.Overdate. Second 8 over 7	Not known	S
91B.	1880/70	Overdate as 91A but no B.P.	Not known	R
91C.	1880	Without B.P.	Not known	R
91D.	1880	Large B.P.	Not known	S
91E.	1880	Small B.P.	Not known	S
92.	1884		1,769,635	N
93.	1885		717,723	S

TYPE IIB. ST.GEORGE SOVEREIGNS OF VICTORIA
(MELBOURNE MINT: MINT MARK M)

NO.	DATE	VARIETIES	MINTAGE	RATING
94.	1872			S
95.	1873		752,199	S
96.	1874			S
97.	1875		1,888,405	N
98.	1876		2,124,445	S
99.	1877		1,487,316	N
100.	1878		2,171,457	C
101.	1879		2,740,594	C
102.	1880			N
103.	1881			N
103A.	1881	Large B.P.	Not known	S
103B.	1881	Without B.P.	Not known	R
104.	1882		2,093,850	N
104A.	1882	Large B.P.		S
105.	1883		1,623,000	N
106.	1884			C
107.	1885			C
108.	1886			C
109.	1887			C
109A.	1887	Large B.P.	Not known	S

Note: See Plate No.30 for variations of B.P.

TYPE IIC ST.GEORGE SOVEREIGNS OF VICTORIA
(SYDNEY MINT: MINT MARK S)

NO.	DATE	VARIETIES	MINTAGE	RATING
*110.	1871			S
110A.	1871	Large B.P.		S
111.	1872			N
112.	1873			N
113.	1874		1,899,000	N
114.	1875			N
115.	1876		1,613,000	S
116.	1879			S
117.	1880			S
117A.	1880	Large B.P.		S
117B.	1880	No B.P.		S
118.	1881			N
118A.	1881	Large B.P.		S
118B.	1881	No B.P.		S
119.	1882			N
119A.	1882	Large B.P.		S
120.	1883			N
121.	1884			N
122.	1885			N
123.	1886			N
124.	1887			N

Where mintage figures are not shown above they are included in the figures previously given for 'shield' sovereigns Type ID of the same mint; separate figures are not known.

*Refer also to 'Note' after Sydney mint 'AUSTRALIA' sovereigns.

At this point I will now include the Sydney branch mint AUSTRALIA Young head sovereigns that were first introduced in 1855 and continued until 1870 (Plate Nos.33 and 34).

Description and details.

First Type bust 1855 and 1856 engraved by James Wyon.
Obverse. Young head of Victoria to left. Hair bound with double fillet and collected into a knot behind.

Legend. VICTORIA D:G:BRITANNIAR:REGINA F:D:

Date below truncation.

Reverse. AUSTRALIA across the centre with a small crown above. A branch of oak leaves on either side joined at the bottom by a knotted bow. ONE SOVEREIGN at the bottom, and SYDNEY MINT displayed at the top.

Edge. Milled.

VICTORIA
SYDNEY BRANCH MINT SOVEREIGNS
(AUSTRALIA) FIRST TYPE

NO.	DATE	VARIETIES	MINTAGE	RATING
360.	1855		502,000	S
361.	1856		981,000	N

Description and details.

Second Type bust 1857 to 1870. Engraver L.C.Wyon.

Observe. Smaller Young head of Victoria to left. The hair is this time bound and collected into a knot behind with a wreath of native Banksia part of which drops down the face, curls below the bottom of the ear, and returns to the knot.

Legend. VICTORIA D:G:BRITANNIAR:REG:F:D:

Date below truncation.

Reverse. As First type.

The coin is struck with a reverse die axis.

Edge. Milled

VICTORIA
SYDNEY BRANCH MINT SOVEREIGNS
(AUSTRALIA) SECOND TYPE

NO.	DATE	VARIETIES	MINTAGE	RATING
362.	1857		499,000	N
363.	1858		1,101,500	N
364.	1859		1,050,500	N
365.	1860		1,573,500	S
366.	1861		1,626,000	N
367.	1862		2,477,500	N
368.	1863		1,255,500	N

Victoria Sydney Branch Mint Sovereigns (Australia) Second Type - contd.

NO.	DATE	VARIETIES	MINTAGE	RATING
369.	1864		2,698,500	N
370.	1865		2,130,500	N
371.	1866		2,911,000	N
372.	1867		2,370,000	N
373.	1868		2,319,000	N
374.	*1869			
375.	1870		1,220,000	N

Note. We know that the Sydney mint often struck sovereigns for a particular year and then continued the same date well into the next year, and also their records failed to indicate which type they were for, therefore mintage figures in general must be looked upon as approximate.

*   No dies were supplied for this year. The mintage figure of 1,202,000 for 1869 has therefore been added to that shown for 1868 on the assumption that the coins continued to be dated 1868.

The next major change in Victoria's coinage was in 1887, and this of course was the fiftieth anniversary of the Queen's accession. The Queen herself agreed to a change of coinage design and Mr J.E.Boehm R.A. was asked to prepare a portrait, and this was accepted by the Queen. Boehm modelled the portrait from life.[1]

Joseph Edgar Boehm, Medallist and Sculptor, was born in Vienna in 1834 and settled in England after 1862, and he was the son of J.D.Boehm the medallist and gem-engraver. The Queen appointed him Sculptor in ordinary in 1881 and he was made a Royal Academician in 1882. In 1889 he was granted a Baronetcy, and he died in 1890.

As a sculptor, Sir Joseph Edgar Boehm, R.A. is known for his very large statues of Queen Victoria at Windsor, John Bunyan at Bedford and the Prince of Wales in Bombay.

Boehm's new effigy of Victoria was adopted for the 'Jubilee' coinage of 1887, and Pistrucci's St.George and Dragon was retained for the reverse. (Plate No.35). However, in spite of the fact Victoria herself had requested a smaller crown and approved the portrait the new obverse design met with much resentment and, ironically, as a result Boehm rapidly fell from grace.

---

1. L.Forrer, *Biographical Dictionary of Medallists*. London Spink and son 1902 Vol1, pp 97-98.

The new 'Jubilee' coinage was struck at the London Mint, and at both branch mints of Melbourne and Sydney. (Plate No.36).

In general these sovereigns are not difficult to obtain, but one coin (M.A.M.125A) dated 1887 from the London Mint may well prove to be a problem. This sovereign displays the initials of J.E.B. engraved very small and with more space between them. A similar variety has been noted on the 1887 sovereigns of the Melbourne and Sydney branch mints, but not quite so tiny as on the London variety. However, all three must be regarded as rare coins. Plate No.37 illustrates some J.E.B. variations.

The branch mint marks for the 'Jubilee' sovereigns of Melbourne and Sydney, a letter M or S, is placed in the centre of the exergue line on the reverse. (Plate No.36).

Description and details.

Obverse. Bust of the Queen facing left wearing small crown, veiled and with ribbon and star of the Garter and the Victoria and Albert Order. The small letters J.E.B. in relief at the bottom of the bust.
Legend. VICTORIA D:G:BRITT:REG:F:D:
Reverse. St.George mounted with streamer flowing from helmet, slaying the dragon with sword. The date is shown below the exergue line with the small letters B.P. to right.
Edge. Milled.

TYPE IIIA. JUBILEE SOVEREIGNS OF VICTORIA
(LONDON MINT: NO MINT MARK)

NO.	DATE	VARIETIES	MINTAGE	RATING
125.	1887		1,111,280	N
125A.	1887	Obv.Very small J.E.B.	Not Known	R2
126.	1888		2,777,424	S
127.	1889		7,267,455	C
128.	1890		6,529,887	C
129.	1891		6,329,476	C
130.	1892		7,104,720	C

TYPE IIIB. JUBILEE SOVEREIGNS OF VICTORIA
(MELBOURNE MINT: MINT MARK M)

NO.	DATE	VARIETIES	MINTAGE	RATING
131.	1887		940,000	S
131A.	1887	Obv.Smaller J.E.B. and with more space between.	Not known	R
132.	1888		2,830,612	N
133.	1889		2,732,590	N
134.	1890		2,473,537	N
135.	1891		2,749,592	N
136.	1892		3,488,750	N
137.	1893		1,649,352	S

TYPE IIIC. JUBILEE SOVEREIGNS OF VICTORIA
(SYDNEY MINT: MINT MARK S)

NO.	DATE	VARIETIES	MINTAGE	RATING
138.	1887		1,002,000	S
138A.	1887	Obv.Smaller J.E.B. and with more space between.	Not known	R
139.	1888		2,187,000	N
140.	1889		3,262,000	C
141.	1890		2,808,000	N
142.	1891		2,596,000	N
143.	1892		2,837,000	N
144.	1893		1,498,000	N

So I come to the final type of Victoria's sovereigns which are known as the 'old head'.

In February 1891 the Chancellor of the Exchequer requested for a committee to meet and then put forward a design for new coinage;[1] this committee of many important dignitaries also included the Deputy Master of the Mint, Mr.C.W.Fremantle, and interestingly Mr.John Evans F.R.S., President of the Numismatic Society.

Following the recommendations of this committee, the Queen accepted

---

1. L.Forrer, *Biographical Dictionary of Medallists*. London Spink & Son 1902 Vol 1, pp 165-166

the design of an effigy by Thomas Brock, R.A., and this would be used on the obverse of all future gold and silver coins. Once again Pistrucci's St.George slaying the dragon was retained for the reverse of the sovereign. (Plate No.38).

Thomas Brock, R.A., was a sculptor of considerable talent and his exhibition at the Royal Academy in 1901 of a beautiful figure of Eve was said by Forrer to be one of his greatest achievements and ranked among the most notable examples of modern sculpture.

Another important event during the last period of Victoria's reign was the opening of the last of Australia's branch mints, and this was the Perth branch in Western Australia. [1] The new Deputy Master was J.F.Campbell and his report to the London Mint of 1 March 1900 stated that the mint buildings were finished by November 1898, and that the erection of machinery etc. was completed in May 1899. After then listing the local deposits of gold received he went on to describe fully the opening of the new branch mint at Perth on 20 June 1899.

The first gold sovereigns to be struck at the Perth branch mint bear the date of 1899.

The branch mint mark for the 'old head' series of Melbourne, Sydney and Perth, a letter M, S or P, is placed in the centre of the exergue line on the reverse. (Plates No.39 and 40).

Description and details.

Obverse. Bust of the Queen facing left, crowned, veiled and draped, wearing ribbon and star of the Garter. The small letters T.B. appear below the bust.
Legend. VICTORIA.DEI.GRA.BRITT.REGINA.FID.DEF.IND.IMP.*
Reverse. St.George slaying dragon as previous type.
Edge. Milled.

* The words IND.IMP. for Empress of India appear in the legend for the first time.

The only coins in the 'old head' series that can be difficult to obtain are the 1899 Perth sovereign (M.A.M.171), and the 1896 Sydney coin (M.A.M.165). However, I must again stress that especially branch mint sovereigns, in top grade, will be very difficult for the collector to find, and so may well be costly.

---

1. J.F.Campbell, 'Perth branch mint report'. *Royal Mint Report* 1899, pp 132-136

TYPE IVA. OLD HEAD SOVEREIGNS OF VICTORIA
(LONDON MINT: NO MINT MARK)

NO.	DATE	VARIETIES	MINTAGE	RATING
145.	1893		6,898,260	C
146.	1894		3,782,611	C
147.	1895		2,285,317	C
148.	1896		3,334,065	C
149.	1898		4,361,347	C
150.	1899		7,515,978	C
151.	1900		10,846,741	C
152.	1901		1,578,948	N

TYPE IVB. OLD HEAD SOVEREIGNS OF VICTORIA
(MELBOURNE MINT: MINT MARK M)

NO.	DATE	VARIETIES	MINTAGE	RATING
153.	1893		1,346,000	N
154.	1894		4,166,874	C
155.	1895		4,165,869	C
156.	1896		4,456,932	C
157.	1897		5,130,565	C
158.	1898		5,509,138	C
159.	1899		5,579,157	C
160.	1900		4,305,904	C
161.	1901		3,987,701	C

TYPE IVC. OLD HEAD SOVEREIGNS OF VICTORIA
(SYDNEY MINT: MINT MARK S)

NO.	DATE	VARIETIES	MINTAGE	RATING
162.	1893		1,346,000	N
163.	1894		3,067,000	C
164.	1895		2,758,000	C
165.	1896		2,544,000	S
166.	1897		2,532,000	C
167.	1898		2,548,000	C
168.	1899		3,259,000	C
169.	1900		3,586,000	C
170.	1901		3,012,000	C

TYPE IVD. OLD HEAD SOVEREIGNS OF VICTORIA
(PERTH MINT: MINT MARK P)

NO.	DATE	VARIETIES	MINTAGE	RATING
171.	1899		690,992	S
172.	1900		1,886,089	N
173.	1901		2,889,333	N

VICTORIA

Plate 11.

Actual Size

Obverse and Reverse of the Type 1A Sovereign No. 22.

Plate 12.

Obverse and Reverse of the Type 1A Sovereign No. 26B. (Overdate 1843/2)

Plate 13.

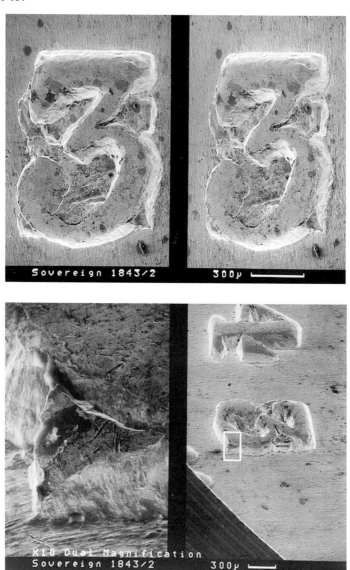

Scanning Microscope photographs. Details of date area Sovereign No. 26B.

Plate 14.

Obverse and Reverse of the Type 1A Sovereign No. 26A. (Narrow shield)

Plate 15.

Obverse and Reverse of the Type 1A Sovereign No. 26. (Yew Tree Hoard)

Plate 16.

Additional Line

Obverse and Reverse of the Type 1A Sovereign No. 42A. (Ansell)

Plate 17.

Obverse and Reverse of the Type 1A Sovereign No. 44A. (Error date)

Plate 18.

Obverse section of the Type 1A Sovereign No. 27A. (Error date)

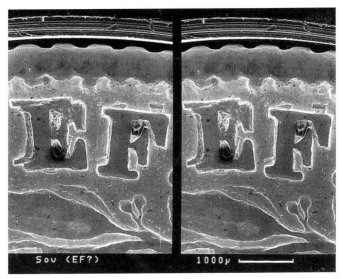

Scanning Microscope photograph of Reverse of the Type 1A Sovereign
No. 45A. (Legend error)

VICTORIA

Plate 19.

827 instead of W.W.

Obverse and Reverse of the Type 1B Sovereign No. 48A. ('827')

Plate 20.

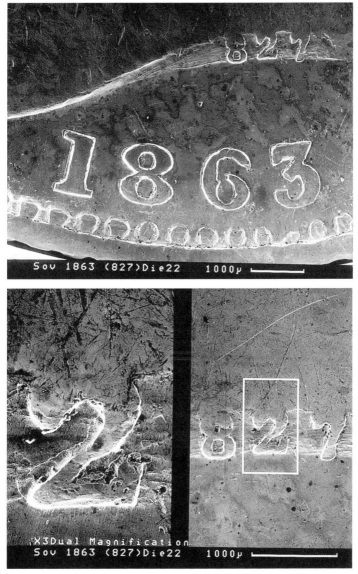

Scanning Microscope photographs for Obverse of Sovereign No. 48A.
(Date area and 827)

Plate 21.

Obverse and Reverse of the Type 1B Sovereign No. 55. (Die Number)

Plate 22.

1.

2.

3.

Obverse and Reverse of the three main groups found within the Type 1A
and Type 1B Series.

Plate 23.

Obverse and Reverse of the Type 1C Melbourne Mint Sovereign No. 61.

Plate 24.

Obverse and Reverse of the Type 1D Sydney Mint Sovereign No. 77.

Plate 25.

Obverse and Reverse of the Type 1C Melbourne Mint Sovereign No.59A.
(Overdate 1872/1)

Scanning Microscope photograph. Detail of date area. No. 59A.

Plate 26.

Actual Size

Obverse and Reverse of the Type 11A London Mint Sovereign No. 90
(1879)

Plate 27.

Obverse and Reverse of the Type 11B Melbourne Mint Sovereign No. 100.

Plate 28.

Obverse and Reverse of the Type 11C Sydney Mint Sovereign No. 119.

Plate 29.

Obverse and Reverse of the Type 11B Melbourne Mint Sovereign No. 103B.
(No BP)

Plate 30.

Date area of Melbourne Mint Sovereign No. 100.
(B.P. similar to London Mint)

Date area of Sydney Mint Sovereign No. 119. (B.P. Slightly smaller)

Date area of London Mint Sovereign No. 84A. (Large B.P.)

Date area of London Mint Sovereign No. 90. (Normal B.P.)

Plate 31.

Obverse and Reverse of the Type 11A London Mint Sovereign No. 91A.
(Overdate 1880/70)

Plate 32.

Scanning Microscope photograph of Sovereign No. 91A. (Full date area 1880/70)

Scanning Microscope photograph of Sovereign No. 91A. (8 over 7)

Plate 33.

Obverse and Reverse of Sydney Branch Mint Sovereign AUSTRALIA
No. 360. (First bust)

Plate 34.

Obverse and Reverse of Sydney Branch Mint Sovereign AUSTRALIA
No. 375. (Second bust)

VICTORIA

Plate 35.

Actual Size

Obverse and Reverse of the Type 111A London Mint Sovereign No. 125.

Plate 36.

Reverse of the Type 111B Melbourne Mint Sovereign No. 133.

Reverse of the Type 111C Sydney Mint Sovereign No. 143.

Plate 37.

Obverse of London Mint Sovereign No. 125. Normal large J.E.B.

Obverse of Melbourne Mint Sovereign No. 131A.
Smaller J.E.B. wider spaced.

Plate 38.

Actual Size

Obverse and Reverse of the Type IVA London Mint Sovereign No. 151.

Plate 39.

Reverse of the Type IVB Melbourne Mint Sovereign No. 153.

Reverse of the Type IVC Sydney Mint Sovereign No. 170.

VICTORIA

Plate 40.

Reverse of the Type IVD Perth Mint Sovereign No. 172.

EDWARD VII 1901-1910

Though Edward VII began his reign in 1901 the new coinage was not introduced until 1902: the gold and silver coins were in fact authorized by Royal Proclamation on 10 December 1901.

The Mint Engraver George William De Saulles had been introduced to the Mint at the end of 1892 in succession to Leonard Wyon.[1] He was apprenticed to Joseph Moore of Birmingham and later worked at Pinches from where he was in fact called to the Mint by the Deputy Master, Sir Charles Fremantle. He modelled and engraved the obverse for the new coinage of Edward VII, and once more Pistrucci's St.George slaying the dragon was retained for the reverse. (Plate No.41). De Saulles exhibited several medals at the Royal Academy Exhibition of 1899, and in general his work was much admired. He died in July 1903.

The latter part of his reign saw the introduction of another branch mint, and this was the new Canadian mint of Ottawa.

In 1900 following the discovery of gold in the Yukon[2], the Canadian Government asked for the right to coin sovereigns, and to achieve this, the new mint that they had already planned would need to be a branch of the Royal Mint.

In 1901 the Canadian House of Commons agreed to fund a branch mint in Ottawa, and this received royal assent. Building of the new mint only began in 1905 and the first sovereigns were not struck until 1908, and then for only two more years to the end of Edward's reign. The branch mint however continued to operate into the reign of George V.

The first Deputy Master for the Ottawa branch mint was James Bonar, and its coins are identified by a letter C placed on the reverse in the centre of the exergue line.

Sovereigns for the reign of Edward VII were struck at the London Mint and the branch mints of Melbourne, Sydney, Perth and Ottawa; the mint marks were a letter M, S, P or C that was placed in the centre of the exergue line on the reverse. (Plates No.43 and 44).

Description and details.

Obverse. The bare head of the King facing right. The small letters DeS (for DeSaulles) below the truncation.

Legend. EDWARDVS VII D:G:BRITT:OMN:REX:F:D:IND:IMP:

---

1. L.Forrer, *Biographical Dictionary of Medallists* London 1901. Vol 1 p 385
2. J.Sharples, 'Sovereigns of the overseas branches' (4) *Royal Sovereign* 1489-1989. p 72

Reverse. St George mounted slaying the dragon, the date below the exergue line with B.P. in small letters to right.
Edge. Milled.

For the collector the sovereigns of neither the London Mint nor the branch mints of Australia will present many problems, although he will still find some difficulty in obtaining really choice examples. However, the new branch mint of Ottawa may well cause big problems. Sovereigns were struck for only three years at the Canadian branch mint and all three dates are extremely rare, but the first of these dated 1908 (M.A.M.183) and (Plate No.42) is without question the rarest. [3]The Deputy Master of the Ottawa branch mint, James Bonar, submitted his report for 1908 on 25 March 1909 to the Royal Mint, and in this report he states that the Melting and Coining Departments struck 678 gold sovereigns for the year 1908. In Appendix B of this report the Statement of the weight and value of gold bullion received for coinage and issued shows that only 633 sovereigns were in fact issued, and they would, as the Statement suggests, have been currency coin. Therefore it is reasonable to suggest that the remaining forty five sovereigns were rejected as being unsuitable for issue.

The specimen sovereign is also extremely rare and my records show just six examples, and for the currency coin I have notes of just four examples in many years. I have been fortunate enough to examine both types, and I firmly believe that the currency sovereign (M.A.M.183) along with the 1819 sovereign (M.A.M.3), are the two rarest sovereigns within the whole series.

EDWARD VII SOVEREIGNS (LONDON MINT: NO MINT MARKS)

NO.	DATE	VARIETIES	MINTAGE	RATING
174.	1902		4,737,796	C
175.	1903		8,888,627	C
176.	1904		10,041,369	C
177.	1905		5,910,403	C
178.	1906		10,466,981	C
179.	1907		18,458,663	C
180.	1908		11,729,006	C
181.	1909		12,157,099	C
182.	1910		22,379,624	C

---

3. J.Bonar, 'Ottawa branch mint report'. *Royal Mint Report* 1908, pp 138-142

EDWARD VII SOVEREIGNS (OTTAWA MINT: MINT MARK C)

NO.	DATE	VARIETIES	MINTAGE	RATING
183.	1908		633	R6
184.	1909		16,300	R2
185.	1910		28,020	R2

EDWARD VII SOVEREIGNS (MELBOURNE MINT: MINT MARK M)

NO.	DATE	VARIETIES	MINTAGE	RATING
186.	1902		4,267,157	C
187.	1903		3,521,780	C
188.	1904		3,743,897	C
189.	1905		3,633,838	C
190.	1906		3,657,853	C
191.	1907		3,332,691	C
192.	1908		3,080,148	C
193.	1909		3,029,538	C
194.	1910		3,054,547	C

EDWARD VII SOVEREIGNS (PERTH MINT: MINT MARK P)

NO.	DATE	VARIETIES	MINTAGE	RATING
195.	1902		4,289,122	C
196.	1903		4,674,783	C
197.	1904		4,506,756	C
198.	1905		4,876,193	C
199.	1906		4,829,817	C
200.	1907		4,972,289	C
201.	1908		4,875,617	C
202.	1909		4,524,241	C
203.	1910		4,690,625	C

EDWARD VII SOVEREIGNS (SYDNEY MINT: MINT MARK S)

NO.	DATE	VARIETIES	MINTAGE	RATING
204.	1902		2,813,000	C
205.	1903		2,806,000	C
206.	1904		2,986,000	C
207.	1905		2,778,000	C
208.	1906		2,792,000	C
209.	1907		2,539,000	C
210.	1908		2,017,000	N
211.	1909		2,057,000	N
212.	1910		2,135,000	N

EDWARD VII

Plate 41.

Actual Size

Obverse and Reverse of the London Mint Sovereign No. 174.

Plate 42.

Obverse and Reverse of the Ottawa Mint Sovereign No. 183. (1908C)

Plate 43.

Reverse of the Melbourne Mint Sovereign No. 192.

Reverse of the Perth Mint Sovereign No. 198.

Plate 44.

Reverse of the Sydney Mint Sovereign No. 209.

Reverse of the Ottawa Mint Sovereign No. 183.

GEORGE V 1910-1936

The year of 1911 saw the issue of the first gold sovereign for George V, and the new bust was the work of Edgar Bertram Mackennal, an Australian born in Melbourne 1863. The reverse for the new coinage was the continuation of Benedetto Pistrucci's St.George slaying the dragon. Plate No.45 illustrates both busts.

[1]Mackennal, who later became Sir Edgar Bertram Mackennal R.A., was a sculptor of considerable talent in both marble and bronze, and he gained many commissions for his work that can be seen in the countries of France, Denmark, India, Australia and England. Among his important work here are the recumbent figures of Edward VII and Queen Alexandra at the Royal Mausoleum at Frogmore, Windsor 1911, a marble portrait of Queen Alexandra for the Sandringham Church in Norfolk 1930, and a statue of Thomas Gainsborough which can be seen at Sudbury in Suffolk. For the coinage of George V he first produced a model from photographs and was then given a special sitting by the King, and he also designed and engraved the Coronation Medal 1910.

Edgar Bertram Mackennal came to England in 1891 and shortly after set up a studio in St.John's Wood, London; then in 1914 he moved to Watcombe Hall near Torquay in Devon and lived there until his death in 1931. He is remembered as a truly great artist, and especially in Australia. After being elected an Associate of the Royal Academy he later became the only Australian to become a full member of the Royal Academy.

The reign of George V created many interesting sovereigns, and indeed happenings, the most dramatic being the outbreak of war in 1914. As a result, the government issued Treasury Notes to the value of £1 and 10s. and with the situation so desperate, the public were asked not to demand gold. In only a short time the new notes took the place of the current gold coinage. However, many more sovereigns were struck during the war years and they became part of the gold reserve held by the Bank of England.

During the war our debts to the United States of America were considerable and there is little doubt that large quantities of sovereigns were used as a payment of these debts. Bearing in mind that the United States were not allowed to hold gold coin as such at that time, it is almost certain that any sovereigns they received would have been melted and made into ingots. Further to this, the Gold Standard Act of 1925 made currency notes no longer exchangeable for gold coins; however, the Bank was compelled to sell to anyone asking for it. The price was £3.17.10 °d per ounce and large quantities were sold. As a result sovereigns worth £91,350,000 were melted during 1929 and 1930; they

---

1. T.M.Pistrucci Archive, *Australian Sculptor*. Ronald Scarlett. (Author's collection)

of course came from the Bank reserve. This, coupled with the United States situation, was undoubtedly the reason why the 1916, 1917 and 1925 sovereigns from the London Mint became rare, though in later years, to the horror of numismatists, the 1925 sovereign was struck again. It is certain that few 1917 coins survived although I have seen four appear in recent years, it is though, still an extremely rare sovereign.

This reign saw the last two branch mints established and the first of these was in India, a country in which His Majesty's Mints had already been operating for several years in Bombay and Calcutta. However, the sovereign had not previously been coined in India, and pending arrangements for the newly proposed mint in Bombay the gold mohur or fifteen rupees piece was in circulation. These coins except for the design were exactly similar to sovereigns, including the weight of 123.27447 grains, and a fineness of eleven twelfths.

[2]The new Bombay branch mint opened in 1918 after building work was completed in May of that year and the dies for coining, plant and machines arrived from London in June. Automatic weighing machines and two coining presses complete with motors arrived from His Majesty's Mint of Bombay in early August.

The first coinage was issued on 15 August 1918, and the new Deputy Master was R.R.Kahan. 1,295,372 sovereigns were struck for that year; although this branch mint continued to operate in 1919 no more sovereigns were struck there.

A proclamation by the King of 14 December 1922 saw the beginning of our last branch mint, this being the Pretoria mint of South Africa.

[3]The new mint was to open officially on 1 January 1923 but because of delays in erecting the machinery and equipping the various departments coining was not possible until some time later during the year.

The new Deputy Master, Mr.R.Pearson, in his report dated 4 February 1924 for the year of 1923 said, "During the period covered by this report only one deposit of gold was received at the mint. This consisted of old jewellery, which after the Rand Refinery's charge for refining, and the Mint charges, was found to be of the net value of £406.0s.9d. The resulting sovereigns were delivered to the depositor."

I wrote to the South African Mint of Pretoria in 1979 and received a reply on 7 February 1980 from the Director of the Suid-Afrikaanse Munt of Pretoria. He confirmed Deputy Master Pearson's report, and also said that the South African Mint collection contained a 1923 currency sovereign;[4] he further stated

---

2. *Royal Mint Report* 1918, 'Bombay branch mint'. Deputy Master R.R.Kahan, pp 144, 145
3. *Royal Mint Report* 1923, 'Pretoria branch mint'. Deputy Master R.Pearson, pp 132-136
4. G.P.Dyer, 'The Existence of 1923 S A Currency Sovereign'. *Spink Numismatic Circular* March 1985, pp 42-43.

that the sovereigns sent to the depositor must have been currency pieces. So the first sovereign of 1923 (M.A.M.287) from the new branch mint of Pretoria is without question an extremely rare piece.

The mint mark for the new Bombay branch mint is the letter I for India, and for the Pretoria branch mint the letters S/A for South Africa. The branch mints of Melbourne, Perth and Sydney plus the Ottawa branch mint also struck sovereigns during this reign and their mint marks, as previously described, are displayed on the reverse of the coin in the centre of the exergue line. (Plates No.46, 47, 48 and 49).

There are two different obverses, the 'small head' type being used for the last three years of the Melbourne and Perth issues and the last four years of the South African issues. (Plate No.45). The large head bust was used for all other sovereigns.

Other points of note I feel worth mentioning in respect of the 'small head' are that on coins I have examined the relief does appear a little less than on Mackennal's larger bust. There are also slight variations on the reverse, and most notable are the tighter folds on the cape; St.George's head appears to be very tight onto the mane of the horse.

Description and details.

Obverse. The King's bare head facing left. The letters B.M. in relief at the bottom of the truncation.
Legend. GEORGIVS V D.G.BRITT:OMN:REX F.D.IND:IMP:
Reverse. St.George mounted and slaying Dragon with sword. Date at the bottom with small letters B.P. to right.
Edge. Milled.

From the London Mint the 1917 coin is by far the rarest and is seldom seen; the 1916 date will perhaps prove a little difficult for most.

All the coins from the Ottawa mint are difficult but that of 1916 (M.A.M.224) will prove a real problem; it is an extremely rare sovereign and could cost the collector in excess of £10,000. The 1913 sovereign is also extremely rare.

There are quite a number of rare sovereigns in the Melbourne series: 1920, 1921, 1922, 1927 and 1928 are the rarest, and all three coins of the 'small head' type are rare.

Of the Perth mint series the most difficult may well prove to be the 1926 sovereign, and several other coins that are rated 'S' will not perhaps be without problems. All of the 'small head' group will not be easy to obtain, especially the 1930 coin.

The Sydney mint has struck six extremely rare sovereigns, and they are the 1920, 1921, 1922, 1923, 1924 and 1926 sovereigns, and to acquire these the collector will need much patience - and cash!

I have already written in detail of the Pretoria mint sovereign of 1923 (M.A.M.287) that does without doubt rate on a par with the 1819 sovereign (M.A.M.3), and the 1908 sovereign (M.A.M.183). The 1924 coin from this branch mint is also an extremely rare piece.

The Bombay branch mint only struck sovereigns for the year 1918, but it should not be difficult to obtain a specimen.

GEORGE V SOVEREIGNS (LONDON MINT: NO MINT MARK)

NO.	DATE	VARIETIES	MINTAGE	RATING
213.	1911		30,044,105	C
214.	1912		30,317,921	C
215.	1913		24,539,672	C
216.	1914		11,501,117	C
217.	1915		20,295,280	C
218.	1916		1,554,120	R
219.	1917		1,014,714	R5
220.	1925*		3,520,431	C

GEORGE V SOVEREIGNS (OTTAWA MINT: MINT MARK C)

NO.	DATE	VARIETIES	MINTAGE	RATING
221.	1911		257,048	S
222.	1913		3,717	R4
223.	1914		14,900	R3
224.	1916		6,119	R5
225.	1917		58,875	R
226.	1918		106,570	S
227.	1919		135,957	S

GEORGE V SOVEREIGNS (BOMBAY MINT: MINT MARK I)

NO.	DATE	VARIETIES	MINTAGE	RATING
228.	1918		1,294,372	N

* 1925 Sovereign (M.A.M.220) refer also to George VI.

GEORGE V SOVEREIGNS (MELBOURNE MINT: MINT MARK M).

NO.	DATE	VARIETIES	MINTAGE	RATING
229.	1911		2,851,451	C
230.	1912		2,469,257	C
231.	1913		2,323,180	C
232.	1914		2,012,029	C
233.	1915		1,637,839	N
234.	1916		1,272,634	N
235.	1917		934,469	S
236.	1918		4,809,493	C
237.	1919		514,257	S
238.	1920		530,266	R2
239.	1921		240,121	R3
240.	1922		608,306	R2
241.	1923		511,129	R
242.	1924		278,140	R
243.	1925		3,311,662	C
244.	1926		211,107	R
245.	1927		310,156	R2
246.	1928		413,208	R2

GEORGE V SOVEREIGNS
MELBOURNE MINT ('SMALL HEAD') MINT MARK M

NO.	DATE	VARIETIES	MINTAGE	RATING
247.	1929		436,938	R3
248.	1930		77,588	R
249.	1931		57,809	R2

GEORGE V SOVEREIGNS (PERTH MINT: MINT MARK P)

NO.	DATE	VARIETIES	MINTAGE	RATING
250.	1911		4,373,165	C
251.	1912		4,278,144	C
252.	1913		4,635,287	C

George V Sovereigns (Perth Mint: Mint Mark P) - contd.

NO.	DATE	VARIETIES	MINTAGE	RATING
253.	1914		4,815,996	C
254.	1915		4,373,596	C
255.	1916		4,096,721	S
256.	1917		4,110,286	S
257.	1918		3,812,884	C
258.	1919		2,995,216	C
259.	1920		2,421,196	C
260.	1921		2,314,360	C
261.	1922		2,298,884	C
262.	1923		2,124,154	C
263.	1924		1,464,416	N
264.	1925		1,837,901	S
265.	1926		1,313,578	R
266.	1927		1,383,544	S
267.	1928		1,333,417	S

GEORGE V SOVEREIGNS
PERTH MINT ('SMALL HEAD') MINT MARK P

NO.	DATE	VARIETIES	MINTAGE	RATING
268.	1929		1,607,625	S
269.	1930		1,915,352	R
270.	1931		1,173,568	S

GEORGE V SOVEREIGNS (SYDNEY MINT: MINT MARK S)

NO.	DATE	VARIETIES	MINTAGE	RATING
271.	1911		2,519,000	C
272.	1912		2,227,000	C
273.	1913		2,249,000	C
274.	1914		1,774,000	C
275.	1915		1,346,000	S
276.	1916		1,242,000	N
277.	1917		1,666,000	C

George V Sovereigns (Sydney Mint: Mint Mark S) - contd.

NO.	DATE	VARIETIES	MINTAGE	RATING
278.	1918		3,716,000	C
279.	1919		1,835,000	N
280.	1920		360,000	R3
281.	1921		839,000	R3
282.	1922		578,000	R3
283.	1923		416,000	R4
284.	1924		394,000	R3
285.	1925		5,632,000	S
286.	1926		1,031,050	R4

GEORGE V SOVEREIGNS
(PRETORIA MINT SOUTH AFRICA) MINT MARK SA

NO.	DATE	VARIETIES	MINTAGE	RATING
287.	1923		406	R6
288.	1924		2,660	R5
289.	1925		6,086,624	C
290.	1926		11,107,611	C
291.	1927		16,379,704	C
292.	1928		18,235,057	C

GEORGE V SOVEREIGNS
PRETORIA MINT ('SMALL HEAD') MINT MARK SA

NO.	DATE	VARIETIES	MINTAGE	RATING
293.	1929		12,024,107	C
294.	1930		10,027,756	C
295.	1931		8,511,792	C
296.	1932		1,066,680	N

Plate 45.

Actual Size

Obverse of the 'Large Head' Sovereign No. 218.

Obverse of the 'Small Head' Sovereign No. 249.

Plate 46.

Actual Size

Reverse of the London Mint Sovereign No. 218.

Reverse of the Melbourne Mint Sovereign No. 249.

96

Plate 47.

Reverse of the Bombay Mint Sovereign No. 228.

Reverse of the Ottawa Mint Sovereign No. 223.

Plate 48.

Reverse of the Sydney Mint Sovereign No. 275.

Reverse of the Perth Mint Sovereign No. 265.

Plate 49.

Reverse of the Pretoria Mint Sovereign No. 295.

Reverse of the Melbourne Mint Sovereign No. 241.

GEORGE VI 1936-1952

Not much can be written concerning the currency sovereigns of George VI as the only sovereigns of this kind struck during the reign were from George V dies that were all dated 1925. Prior to this the 1925 sovereign had been somewhat scarce, and so it is easy to imagine the dismay this must have caused numismatists at that time.

The only sovereign bearing the bust of George VI is dated 1937 and is a specimen coin with plain edge, and it was struck to commemorate the Coronation. The effigy on the obverse was modelled by Mr.T.H.Paget from a personal sitting, and the reverse displays Pistrucci's St.George slaying the Dragon. (Plate No.50).

Description and details.

Obverse. The bare head of the King to the left. The small letters H.P. standing for Humphrey Paget below truncation at rear.
Legend. GEORGIVS VI D:G:BR:OMN:REX F:D:IND:IMP.
Reverse. St.George with streamer from helmet, mounted and slaying the dragon with sword. Date below exergue line with B.P. to right.
Edge. Plain.
The coin is struck to proof standard 'with mirror-like' fields.

The George V currency sovereigns all of which were dated 1925 struck during the reign of George VI are:

NO.	DATE STRUCK	MINTAGE
220	1949	138,000*
220	1951	318,000*
220	1952	430,000*

The sovereigns numbered 220 above are the same as those listed as No.220 in the reign of George V.

* These figures have not been included in the mintage given for sovereign No.220 of George V.

GEORGE VI

Plate 50.

Actual Size

Obverse and Reverse of the 1937 Proof Sovereign

101

ELIZABETH II ACC. 1952

Queen Elizabeth II succeeded her father on 6 February 1952 and to date we have seen five different busts of the Queen and all have been the work of excellent sculptors. The first and second busts were the work of Mary Gillick and she was granted personal sittings by the Queen, the third bust was by Arnold Machin, and the fourth bust is the work of Raphael David Maklouf, for which he was granted personal sittings by the Queen. The last and fifth bust is by the Sculptor and Medallist, Ian Rank-Broadley, and he worked from photographs taken specially for coinage purposes by permission of Her Majesty. The reverse for these five different issues all display Benedetto Pistrucci's St.George slaying the dragon.

I have not yet included that most important issue, the 500th anniversary sovereign 1489-1989. This splendid proof coin, celebrating the remarkable history of the gold sovereign, is the work of Bernard Sindall.

The decision to adopt a decimal currency system was announced in March 1966, and the introduction of the new coinage was scheduled for 15 February 1971. It was obvious that the Royal Mint facilities at Tower Hill would not enable them to cope with the demands of the new coinage, and indeed it brought to an end centuries of minting in London when the Government decided to build a new Mint in Llantrisant, South Wales.

I can well remember the grand old Mint building at Tower Hill that had been used by the Royal Mint for the last 150 years and I visited it many times during the past years.[1] It was designed by the Mint architect James Johnson who died in 1807, and Sir Robert Smirke took over the work and this truly magnificent Georgian building was finished in 1811, the keys being formally handed to the Constable in August 1812. How wonderful it is for me to conclude this part by telling you that the very last coin to be struck at the Royal Mint, Tower Hill, was a gold sovereign bearing the date 1974 and was struck on 10 November 1975.

Our Queen has always shown a keen interest in our coinage and its minting, and on 17 December 1968 the new Royal Mint at Llantrisant was officially opened by Her Majesty.

In 1982 another great occasion was honoured by the presence of Her Majesty and I refer to the Trial of the Pyx. The Trial is held annually and in 1982 it marked the 700th anniversary of this very ancient ceremony. Her Majesty's gracious presence at Goldsmiths Hall on 25 February 1982 for the ceremony was itself an historic occasion being the very first time a reigning Queen had attended this ceremony.

---

1. Sir John Craig, K.C.V.O. C.B. L.L.D. *The Mint* 1953, pp 270 and 271 pp 394-407.

The Trial of the Pyx in fact refers to the box in which samples are locked up. These Trials are held every year and their purpose is to provide an independent check on the accuracy of composition, weight and fineness of the coins minted in the previous year. The law defines that the Mint must set aside for trial one in every two thousand gold coins minted, then having been sworn in by the Queen's Remembrancer, the Trial jury that consists of Freemen of the Goldsmiths Company take from each packet whatever coins they deem necessary. The coins are then individually weighed and melted into an ingot to be later assayed. The remaining coins are weighed in bulk from which the jury selects as many coins as they think necessary; these are weighed and assayed individually. The Trial is then adjourned for a few weeks while assaying is carried out, finally on a new given date the jury re-assembles in Goldsmiths Hall and the verdicts are read by the Clerk of the Company. Normally the Chancellor of the Exchequer is in attendance.

The first sovereign struck in this reign was a proof coin dated 1953 and only a few were struck for the National collections. The new obverse is by Mary Gillick. (Plate No.51).

Description and details. (Proof issue only)

Obverse. Bare head of the Queen facing right, with tie at the back of the hair, the letters MG incuse at the bottom of the bust.
Legend. ELIZABETH II DEI GRA:BRITT:OMN:REGINA F:D:+
Reverse. St.George with streamer flowing from helmet, mounted and slaying the Dragon with a sword. Date below exergue line with the small letters B.P. to the right.
Edge. Milled.

In 1957 the first currency type sovereign for the reign was struck and the new second issue bust was again the work of Mary Gillick (Plate No.52). The title BRITT.OMN., has now been omitted from the Queen's titles owing to the changing status of many Commonwealth territories.

Description and details. (Currency issue)

Obverse. Bare head of the Queen facing right with tie at the back of hair, the letters M.G. incuse at bottom of bust.
Legend. ELIZABETH.II.DEI.GRATIA.REGINA.F:D:+
Reverse. St.George with streamer flowing from helmet mounted and slaying the Dragon with a sword. Date below exergue line with the small letters B.P. to right.
Edge. Milled. The edge milling on the 1957 sovereign is slightly less coarse than the other issues of the series.

ELIZABETH II SOVEREIGNS (SECOND ISSUE)

NO.	DATE	VARIETIES	MINTAGE	RATING
297.	1957	(Finer edge graining)	2,072,000	N
298.	1958		8,700,000	C
299.	1959		1,385,228	N
300.	1962		3,000,000	C
301.	1963		7,400,000	C
302.	1964		3,000,000	C
303.	1965		3,800,000	C
304.	1966		7,050,000	C
305.	1967		5,000,000	C
306.	1968		4,203,000	C

In 1974 a new bust of the Queen was introduced for the third issue and it was the work of the sculptor Arnold Machin. The Queen is shown wearing a tiara (Plate No.53).

Description and details. (Currency issue)

Obverse. Bust of the Queen facing right and wearing a coronet.
Legend. ELIZABETH.II.DEI.GRATIA.REGINA.F:D:
Reverse. St.George with streamer flowing from helmet, mounted and slaying Dragon with sword. Date below exergue line with small letters B.P. to right.
Edge. Milled.

ELIZABETH II SOVEREIGNS (THIRD ISSUE DECIMAL PERIOD)

NO.	DATE	VARIETIES	MINTAGE	RATING
307.	1974		5,002,566	C
308.	1976		4,045,056	C
309.	1978		6,555,000	C
310.	1979		9,100,000	C
311.	1980		5,100,000	C
312.	1981		5,000,000	C
313.	1982		2,950,000	C

The fourth issue saw the introduction of the third new portrait of the Queen and the new effigy was designed by Raphael David Maklouf (Plate No.54).

The first sovereigns bearing the new bust were dated 1985 and they were struck for every year up to and including 1997. All are proof coins.

Description and details. (Fourth issue) Proof sovereigns only

Obverse. Bust of the Queen facing right and wearing a diadem, the letters RDM on the truncation.
Legend. ELIZABETH II DEI.GRA.REG.F.D.
Reverse. St.George with streamer flowing from helmet, mounted and slaying Dragon with a sword. Date below the exergue line with the small letters B.P. to right.
Edge. Milled.

In the year 1989 a special proof sovereign was struck to mark the 500th anniversary of the sovereign 1489-1989 (Plate No.55). I really believe this lovely sovereign is a splendid example of both design and engraving; it is the work of sculptor Bernard Sindall. The obverse features the enthroned effigy of the Queen seated, wearing a crown and robed in superb regal splendour. On the reverse the Royal Arms are placed in the centre of a large Tudor rose with the crown above, and on both sides the inscription shown in Tudor-style lettering. The coin's edge is milled.

So to bring us up to date we have arrived at 1998, and in this year the fifth bust was introduced. The new effigy is the work of sculptor and medallist, Ian Rank-Broadley. (Plate No 56)

The new sovereign is issued as a proof coin only and continues into this year.

Description and details. (Fifth issue) Proof sovereigns only.

Obverse. Bust of the Queen facing right and wearing a tiara, the letters IRB below the truncation.
Legend. ELIZABETH.II.DEI.GRA REGINA.FID.DEF
Reverse. St.George with streamer flowing from helmet, mounted and slaying Dragon with a sword.
Date below exergue line with small letters B.P. to right.
Edge. Milled.

Note. Colour Plates for the reign of Elizabeth II. Courtesy of the Royal Mint.

Plate 51.

Actual Size

Obverse and Reverse of the 1953 Proof Sovereign

Plate 52.

Obverse and Reverse of the 'Second' Issue Sovereign No. 297.

Plate 53.

Obverse and Reverse of the 'Third' Issue Sovereign No. 310.

Plate 54.

Obverse and Reverse of the 'Fourth' Issue Proof Sovereign 1985

Plate 55.

Obverse and Reverse of the special issue Proof Sovereign.
(500th Anniversary 1489-1989)

Plate 56.

Obverse and Reverse of the 'Fifth' Issue Proof Sovereign 1998

FINALLY

Over a period of many years I have sought for and studied the gold sovereign, probably the world's best known of all gold coins, and during this time I have come by a number of other 'objects' which are very much associated with it. I will tell you something about these other objects that to me have also proved so fascinating.

The first of these is the Sovereign Case. It is usually a beautifully made piece, often by a professional Gold or Silversmith, and so hallmarked and with the maker's initials. The purpose was of course to contain gold sovereigns, this being achieved by means of a spring pushing upwards on to a disc the size of the coin, the coins being held between the two by means of a rim round about two-thirds of the edge. Most cases hold up to six sovereigns in a single compartment, and I have seen cases with from one to five compartments. These cases were often carried on the end of a watch albert and so in the waistcoat pocket.

Sovereign cases can be found made from various metals including 18ct and 9ct gold, silver, silverplate, nickel silver, gun metal, leather and even wood. I have seen a case made of rosewood with a secret compartment that has a screw top and pushes in. It holds ten sovereigns (Plate No.57). Also shown on this plate is a unique Swiss watch/sovereign/card holder case complete with pencil, a silver sovereign case that fits onto a cane, it holds five sovereigns, and a gold sovereign/vesta case, it has a Chester hallmark of 1908 and was made by William Nathan. This case has a value of £500.

These days single silver cases cost around £100-£150, and double or treble cases £150-£350 (Plate No.58). A gold combination case will be upward of £500 (Plate No.57). These are becoming more difficult to find but the odd one does occasionally appear at Antique Fairs and in shops of the same nature.

Sovereign Balances and Weights. These lovely balances and weights were used by shopkeepers, and also by travellers. The balance (Plate No.59), although not looking like a piece of precision engineering, was in fact very accurate and the shopkeeper would always have a set on his counter to check if the sovereign was light in weight. When the coin was placed on the platter, if the weight was correct then it would just slightly tip the balance. There was also a slot in the centre of the platter through which the coin should just pass. These balances were made of brass and with two platters, one for the sovereign and the other for the half-sovereign, and most also have the maker's name. All are stamped with the crown, and they were originally supplied in small red cardboard boxes with a green label. These little balances date around the 1830 period and do still appear now and again. However, you will indeed be very fortunate to find one with its original cardboard box. Overleaf is a copy of the green label shown on W.BLEW'S box (Plate No.59).

W.BLEW'S Improved Sovereign Balance
To weigh and gauge Sovereigns and half sovereigns
Being so exact that no counterfeit can possibly go through the gauge
of sufficient weight to turn the balance.

These balances today cost around £40 if in nice condition and probably £50 if you are lucky and find it still with its case.

The next balance is more sophisticated and is known as an Automatic Sovereign Balance (Plate No.59). The maker was R.Brown & Co., Prescot, Lancashire. It dates about 1850 and is much more advanced than the first balance I described. This balance is contained in a very thin but elegant mahogany box and is made of brass and is collapsible, in such a way that when the lid of the box is fully opened the balance is brought up out of the box into an operational position. The end of the bar carries a brass sleeve which can be turned over along the bar so that half-sovereigns can be weighed - the first position being for full sovereigns. There is a movable slide on the weighing side of the bar, being for weight adjustment, and the tray which holds the coin is hinged and hangs down from the bar end. This type of balance is a very well crafted piece and was used by merchants and other businessmen who would have been involved in sovereign transactions. Balances of this kind are very difficult to find these days and a good example might well exceed £300.

The coin weight is something else I have found over the years that has brought considerable interest to me, more than likely because of its affinity to the gold sovereign! [1]The brass coin-like pieces were (Plate No 58) introduced to assist merchants or indeed anyone who wanted to check the weight of his gold coins, and even the modern period has produced a very large number of them. There are as one would expect some bearing the name of the Royal Mint, and many others including some made by established scalemakers.

Most of the coin weights for the sovereign are round and about the size of the real coin, but a good deal thicker, and some can be found uniface. I have seen those named ROYAL MINT with the lion passant over crown and dated 1821, a similar variety of 1824 and a further variety without the lion passant over crown, but with Victoria to the left. It is dated 1843.

Some of the other makers whose work I have seen are W. & T.Avery, W.Chambers Day and I.C.Ratcliffe. I know of two Irish makers, S.Gatchell & Sons, and James Pickering. Some of these use nice floral designs on the obverse, and I have seen another that features an attractive beehive, dated 1843.

Nearly all weights display the weight 5 DWT 2° GRS for the sovereign, and 2 DW 13$\frac{1}{8}$ GR for the half sovereign, and most have the words CURT WEIGHT with the denomination of ONE SOVEREIGN or HALF SOVEREIGN as the case may be. I am sure many will find weights of real

---

1. P and B.Withers, *British Coin Weights*. Llanfyllin, Powys 1993.

interest, and they do cover a wide area; another important fact is that they are not too costly.

Now to conclude I must mention counterfeit sovereigns; alas they do exist. There are many counterfeits around these days; I have seen them of every reign and some have been extremely good reproductions and others very poor. It does seem that forgers are becoming a great deal more accomplished, especially I believe because of the advancement of modern technology.

I mention a few points that may help you if you are confronted with a possible forgery:

The colour is often too yellow and gives a hazy-like impression. Check the weight and study the design and bust very carefully; what at first glance appears to be wear may well be weakness in parts of the striking, which is often one of the major faults of the counterfeit; another is the field of the coin which should be very flat and without a blemish. In this area the counterfeit often has marks and indentations that should not be present. Check also mint marks carefully; I have seen sovereigns with an incorrect mint mark and others with a mint mark that should not have been present at all. Look carefully at the St.George and Dragon design; I have seen this when the streamer should not have been flowing from the helmet.

I have mentioned several examples to look for, and here are four more sovereigns that I actually have in my own counterfeit collection. The first is a silver-gilt coin of 1822, another similar piece dated 1820, an excellent gold copy of a 1917 Perth mint sovereign, and the final piece is a platinum-gilt copy dated 1872 die number 29.[1] These pieces were all examined by the International Bureau for the Suppression of Counterfeit Coins, whose Consultant Director was E.G.V.Newman O.B.E, B.Sc., F.R.I.C. Vincent Newman for many years, until last year when he sadly passed away, had worked tirelessly with Graham Dyer of the Royal Mint to thwart the counterfeiter, and over a period of many years Vincent became a personal friend who examined many sovereigns for me.

I hope what I have written on counterfeits will be helpful to you. However, if you are in any doubt about the genuineness of a sovereign you can always send it to the Royal Mint where I know Mr.G.P.Dyer will be pleased to advise.

So I have reached the end of this second edition of *The Gold Sovereign* and I hope you will enjoy and find of real value what I have written about our most famous gold coin. I make no apology for concluding in the same way as before:

The King of Britain's gold goes marching on. How good it is that marching on also is that most famous reverse of all - Pistrucci's St.George and Dragon. Genius has survived.

---

1. G.P.Dyer, *International Bureau for the Suppression of Counterfeit Coins*, Vol 8. °. London 1983, pp 49-51

Plate 57.

A gold Sovereign/Vesta case by
William Nathan. Chester 1908.

A unique Watch/Sovereign/Card
case Swiss Regd. by Rodolphe
Uhlmann 1903.

A Rosewood Sovereign case with
secret compartment

A rare silver Sovereign case for a
cane top. London 1895

Plate 58.

A rare Sovereign case by William
Nathan. Hallmark Chester 1906

A handsome unique silver
Sovereign case for six coins.
Hallmark London 1885.

Uniface Victorian Sovereign weight.

Obverse and Reverse of a scarce
Dublin Sovereign weight.

Uniface Sovereign weight 1842.

Plate 59.

Sovereign Balance made by W. Blew complete with original cardboard box.

Automatic Sovereign Balance made by R. Brown & Co.
in mahogany folding case.

SELECT BIBLIOGRAPHY

G.F. Ansell *The Royal Mint*, 3ʳᵈ edition (London, 1871)

C.E.Challis (ed) *A New History of the Royal Mint*, (Cambridge University Press, 1992)

Sir John Craig *The Mint*, A History of the London Mint from A.D.287 to 1948 (Cambridge, 1953)

J.J.Cullimore Allen *Sovereigns of the British Empire*, (London, 1965)

Sir Geoffrey Duveen and H.G.Stride *The History of the Gold Sovereign,* (London, 1962)

Captain K.J.Douglas-Morris, R.N. *Distinguished Collection of English Gold Coins* 1700-1900, Sotherby & Co Sale Catalogue, Nov 1974

L.Forrer *Biographical Dictionary of Medallists,* Vol I Spink & Son (London, 1902)

P.Grierson The Origins of the English Sovereign and the Symbolism of the Closed Crown, *British Numismatic Journal*, 1964

R.L.Kenyon *The Gold Coins of England*, (London, 1884)

M.A.Marsh *The Gold Sovereign,* 1ˢᵗ edition (Cambridge, 1980)

M.A.Marsh *The Gold Half Sovereign,* 1ˢᵗ edition (Cambridge, 1982)

M.A.Marsh *Benedetto Pistrucci Principal Engraver & Chief Medallist of The Royal Mint,* 1783-1855, 1ˢᵗ edition (Cambridge, 1996)

Royal Mint *Annual Report of the Deputy Master and Comptroller,* 1870-1977

Royal Mint *Royal Sovereign* 1489-1989 (Royal Mint Cardiff, 1989)

Col J.T.Smith *Remarks on a Gold Currency for India and Proposal of Measures for the Introduction of the British Sovereign,* (London, 1868)